Author: Milos Bogdanovic,
  mishabogdanovic@gmail.com
  +381 (0)64 15 15 092

Milos Bogdanovic

Infiltration of Jesuitism into Modern Protestantism and Popular Psychology

From Ignatius Loyola to Jon Dybdahl

"Fear God, and give Him glory, because the hour of His judgment has come; worship Him who made the heaven and the earth and sea and springs of waters. And another angel, a second one, followed, saying, Fallen, fallen is Babylon the great, she who has made all the nations drink of the wine of the passion of her immorality." (Revelation 14:7-8)

"And these also reel with wine and stagger from strong drink: The priest and the prophet reel with strong drink, They are confused by wine, they stagger from strong drink; They reel while having visions, They totter when rendering judgment." (Isaiah 28:7)

"Behold, the Lord has a strong and mighty agent; As a storm of hail, a tempest of destruction, Like a storm of mighty over-flowing waters, He has cast it down to the earth with His hand. The proud crown of the drunkards of Ephraim is trodden under foot." (Isaiah 28:2-3)

FOREWORD

During the XX century, the decadence of the Western world into hedonism also imbued modern Protestantism. The principle of Protestantism - *"Only Scripture"* was replaced with the principle - *"Only my feelings! Only my Ego!"* Various self-deceiving techniques, against which Protestantism arose in the 16th century, have again become actual, either under the form of contemporary religion, or under the form of contemporary psychology. The result of accepting Jesuit's delusions is the fact that many Protestants no longer see any reason for the protest, and since they themselves advocate the Jesuit's delusions, they are not aware of what against they should protest. Those who, however, continue to criticize Jesuitism, usually do it extremely superficially, dealing with its intentions, but incapable of reprimanding its delusions. The most tragic consequence of Jesuit's delusions is the suffocated awareness of one's own spiritual need, the absence of healthy self-criticism, and the throwing of responsibility for the bad fruits of their spirit to stressful situations and childhood traumas. This book is a response to the need to unmask Jesuit's delusions and their self-deceiving techniques which today many people apply in search of that peace that only God can bestow on them through all the simplicity of the neglected Gospel. This book also presents a critical analysis of some psychological techniques applied by atheists, so it can be interesting and useful to them, regardless of the occasional use of spiritual terms.

TERM AND MEANING OF SPIRITUAL FORMATION

The term "Spiritual formation" is the term that represents man's spiritual forming and transformation. But between spiritual formation and transformation, represented by the Spiritual formation movement and represented by the Bible, there are essential differences.

As I will explain below, the Spiritual formation directs the human mind to egocentric dwelling upon himself and his own feelings, thus awakening his own self-righteous motives, instead of directing the mind to dwell upon God and His exalted character, which would naturally result in the transformation of essential motives of the fallen human nature.

Because of the neglected conception of the requirements of God's law, the representative of the Spiritual formation repents only for the unpleasant consequences of sin in his thoughts, feelings and actions, but not for the sinful motives of his own heart. That is why after the repentance - he sins again. Because of the neglected focus on Christ and the neglected conception of God's love, the strength of his repentance is not based upon God's love, but upon motives and emotions of his own nature that is void of new birth (upon fear of unclean conscience, pride and selfish sentiment).

Instead of achieving a reform of the heart motives, he deceives himself with the experience of the reform of his own feelings. Since he doesn't have peace from God, he tries to achieve it alone, by the psychological effect of his exercises and rituals.

Being unrepentant for their sins, the believers cannot have peace with God or be satisfied with forgiveness of sins promised by God, and therefore they are trying to achieve the inner peace on their own merits, performing the various techniques and good deeds.

The most common ways of satisfying the unclean conscience among representatives of the Spiritual formation are confession of sins to another person, blaming of parents and other people for their own sins, and inebriating with emotion of being loved, by which the awareness of spiritual emptiness is suffocated. A believer who truly repented of his sins would have a clear conscience without having to pacify his conscience using additional techniques. His righteous life would be the consequence of relying on God, not on the technique by which he substitutes God.

The concept of the Spiritual formation will become clearer to us if we take into account the causes of its origin, which originate from the "Spiritual Exercises" of Ignatius Loyola, the leader of the Catholic counter-reformation.

THE ORIGIN OF SPIRITUAL FORMATION - CATHOLIC COUNTER-REFORMATION

When the Protestant Reformation arose, it brought great novelties in people's lives, and made Protestant nations visibly blessed in comparison to Catholics. The Catholic counter-reformation tried to cause the same changes among its believers, but instead of spiritual rebirth, it tried to accomplish it by repression and manipulation. Seeing that Protestants are willing to sacrifice their lives for their Lord, the leader of the counter-reformation, Ignatius Loyola, founded the movement of the Jesuits, ready for the very same zeal for their Catholic faith. However, their zeal is not based on trusting in God and accepting His righteousness, but on arousing the fanatic motives of human nature itself. This excitement of fanatical motives is achieved by the techniques which Ignatius Loyola published in his work "Spiritual Exercises".

Although Loyola divided his spiritual exercises into several different phases, we can notice two stages of exercises, different in their function. The first phase of exercises (the first week) has the purpose to set in motion fanatical motives of human nature - the fear of unclean conscience, pride and sentiment, as drivers of religious zeal. The second phase of the exercises (the remaining three weeks) has the purpose, by sensual and emotional sensations (imagination and mystical experience), to suffocate the unpleasant symptoms of the initiated fanatical motives of human nature from the first phase. Both phases involve the confession of sins, but in a different function: in the first phase - for the burdening with guilt, and in the second - for psychological satisfaction. Both phases are woven into the 12 steps of Anonymous Alcoholics program, and various other modern programs of working on ourselves.

These phases are contrary to the teaching of the Scriptures, where God first reveals his love for a man, and only after that, He rebukes him for his sins, so that man's repentance and zeal would be based on God's love for a man, and not on injured personal self-righteousness (guilt, embarrassment and sorrow of selfish sentiment).

God first discovers Himself as worthy of trust, reveals His love by liberating the Jews from the Egyptian or Babylonian bondage, and only then He introduces the requirements of the law, so that their repentance would be the fruit of the knowledge of God's love, and not the hurt personal self-righteousness. When the Israelites came out of the Babylonian bondage, they bitterly cried listening to the demands of the laws that they broke and the revelations of God's guardianship that they had so far despised ungratefully. Then the priests "said to all the people, This day is holy to the LORD your God; do not mourn or weep. For all the people were weeping when they heard the words of the law.

Then he said to them, Go, eat of the fat, drink of the sweet, and send portions to him who has nothing prepared; for this day is holy to our Lord. Do not be grieved, for the joy of the LORD is your strength." (Nehemiah 8:9-10)

If the people, aware of their real guilt, continued to surrender to their sorrow and feelings of guilt, their decision to repent would be forced and hypocritical. As soon as this feeling was later relieved, they would fall into sin again. And this is how love and gratitude to God and neighbor become the power that keep them eternally from sin.

While it is realistic that a person feels guilt, sorrow and shame for their sins, these feelings must never become the driving force behind repentance, for they will only produce the suppression of sin in the subconscious and hypocrisy.

The power for repentance should be only the true selfless love, which we do not find in ourselves, but in God, through the proper knowledge of God and reliance on Him. The Bible warns us against the arousing of the motives of one's own nature in the path of repentance:

"And the Lord said: Because this people draw near with their mouth and honor me with their lips, while their hearts are far from me, and their fear of me is a commandment taught by men, therefore, behold, I will again do wonderful things with this people, with wonder upon wonder..." (Isaiah 29:13-14)

"There is no fear in love; but perfect love casts out fear, because fear involves punishment, and the one who fears is not perfected in love." (1 John 4:18)

"For God hath not given us the spirit of fear; but of power, and of love, and of a sound mind." (2 Timothy 1:7)

"Or do you think lightly of the riches of His kindness and tolerance and patience, not knowing that the kindness of God leads you to repentance?" (Romans 2:4)

FIRST PHASE - INDUCEMENT OF FANATICAL MOTIVES OF HUMAN NATURE AS MOTIVES OF RELIGIOUS ZEAL

INDUCEMENT OF THE FEAR OF UNCLEAN CONSIENCE:

By a spiritual exercise consisting of the imagining how our own body tortures in hell for our own guilt, aroused is the fear of an unclean conscience as a trigger for repentance and religious zeal. *"The second consists in asking for an intimate perception of the punishments which the damned undergo; ... The first point is, to see by the imagination the vast fires of hell, and the souls inclosed in certain fiery bodies, as it were in dungeons. The second, to hear in imagination the lamentations, the howlings, the exclamations, and the blasphemies against Christ and His saints, thence breaking forth. The third, to perceive by the smell also of the imagination, the smoke, the brimstone, and the stench of a kind of sink or filth, and of putrefaction. The fourth, to taste in like manner those most bitter things, as the tears, the rottenness, and the worm of conscience."* (The Spiritual Exercises of St. Ignatius of Loyola, 87) ... The person is required to burden himself with guilt and to look at himself *"to be a kind of ulcer or boil, from which so great and foul a flood of sins, so great a pestilence of vices, has flowed down."* (The Spiritual Exercises of St. Ignatius of Loyola, 83)

INDUCEMENT OF THE SHAME OF THE INSULTED ARROGANCE: With the next spiritual exercise, the shame of the insulted arrogance is aroused, as a trigger for repentance and religious zeal: *"The second, that, when awake, immediately excluding all other thoughts, I apply my mind to that which I am about to contemplate in the first exercise, the exercise of midnight; and that, for the sake of the greater shame and confusion, I set before me an example of this kind : how some soldier might stand before his king and the court, ashamed, anxious, and confounded ; having been convicted of having grievously offended against the king himself, from whom he had previously received very many and great favours and presents."* (The Spiritual Exercises of St. Ignatius of Loyola, 90)

INDUCEMENT OF THE SORROW OF THE SELFISH SENTIMENT: Next spiritual exercise evokes the sadness of a selfish sentiment. This sentiment serves as a trigger for repentance and religious zeal: *"The fourth, to consider what Christ our Lord is suffering in His humanity, or seeking to suffer; according to the point taken for meditation : whence let me begin myself also to excite in myself with tlie greatest efforts, grief, sorrow, and weeping; and I shall take care of the same thing in the points that follow. The fifth, to meditate how the Divinity of Christ hides Itself; and, though able, destroys not His enemies, but permits His humanity to suffer such cruel punishments. The sixth, to con-*

sider, when He bears such things for my sins, what I ought to do or suffer for His sake." (The Spiritual Exercises of St. Ignatius of Loyola, 133)

SECOND PHASE - MAN SUFFOCATES THE UNWANTED SYMPTOMS OF THE EVOKED FANATICAL MOTIVES OF HIS NATURE

When in the first phase of spiritual exercises people incite the fear of an unclean conscience, pride and selfish sentiment as their driving motives, then these motives result in unpleasant side effects.

The fear of an unclean conscience makes a person suspicious (fearful of conspiracy), prone to condemning others and unable to accept other people as they are. Arrogance makes the person too sensitive of insults, resentful and prone to violence. Selfish sentiment makes the person emotionally hypersensitive, vulnerable and depressive.

Lest such person, on the basis of the natural symptoms of unclean conscience, arrogant offensiveness and emotional vulnerability, becomes aware of the true nature of her driving motives, Ignatius Loyola, in his "Spiritual Exercises," offers the exercises of imagination by which the person, with all her "five senses", experiences such sensations, which will suffocate her awareness of the true nature of the motives that have been aroused by the exercises of the previous phase: *"After the preparatory prayer, with the three already mentioned preludes, it is eminently useful to exercise the five imaginary senses concerning the first and second contemplations in the following way, according as the subject shall bear. The first point will be, to see in imagination all the persons, and, noting the circumstances which shall occur concerning them, to draw out what may be profitable to ourselves. The second, by hearing as it were what they are saying, or what it may be natural for them to say, to turn all to our own advantage. The third, to perceive by a certain inward taste and smell, how great is the sweetness and delightfulness of the soul imbued with the divine gifts and virtues, according to the nature of the person we are considering, adapting to ourselves those things which may bring us some fruit. The fourth, by an inward touch to handle and kiss the garments, places, foot-steps, and other things connected with such persons ..."* (The Spiritual Exercises of St. Ignatius of Loyola, 56-57)

If the first phase of the exercises would be analogous to taking parasites into the organism, the second phase of the exercises would be analogous to **taking anesthetics**, so that a man would not be aware that he is full of parasites.

While in his heart he retains guilt, pride, selfishness, and perhaps hatred as his initiators of religious zeal, a man, through appropriate spiritual exercises, suffocates the symptoms of his bad motives at the level of feelings - he suffocates the feeling of guilt, the feeling of hatred, etc.

Besides the method of sensual sensations, exercises of the Ignatius Loyola give a person a psychological satisfaction by which he liberates himself from the feeling of guilt through confessing the sins to another man and through the psychological effect of repetition of prayers, etc. That the concept of prayer itself does not represent a real conversation with God, but only a ritual in which people seek satisfaction, reveals a spiritual exercise that represents a combination of prayer with breathing technique: *"The second is, that he who shall wish to spend more time in praying to measure, may say all the aforesaid prayers, or part of them; observing the same order of breathing to measure, as it has been explained."* (The Spiritual Exercises of St. Ignatius of Loyola, 229)

When people do not seek salvation in God, the unsatisfied thirst of the soul remains, and burdens them with the unsatiated need for satisfaction which they seek outside of God: *"The sixth, to praise moreover relics, the veneration and invocation of Saints : [Autograph, to praise the relics of the Saints, giving to the one (the relics) veneration, and addressing prayer to the other (the Saints)] : also the stations, and pious pilgrimages, indulgences, jubilees, the candles accustomed to be lighted in the Churches, and the other helps of this kind to our piety and devotion. [Autograph, jubilees, crusades, and the candles accustomed to be lighted in the Churches.]* " (The Spiritual Exercises of St. Ignatius of Loyola, 176)

Since a person who is offensive, emotionally vulnerable and suspicious, is not capable for social life, he has a need for the loneliness that a monastic life provides for him. Encounter with the temptations of everyday life would easily show that he builds his spiritual building on sand, and not on Rock, because everyday temptations would ruin this building.

Ignatius Loyola advocates that loneliness from friends, other people and jobs, yields many benefits, explaining that in this way an uninterrupted service to God is achieved, as is not interfered with other people (Ignatius Loyola, Spiritual Exercises, 14).

In order not to make the person aware of his own self-deception, he is banned from the spirit of critique, discussion and re-examination. Of all her spiritual authorities, he must think and speak only positive. Towards the community itself, he forms a cult relationship, so if his spiritual authority *"defined anything to be black which to our eyes appears to be white, we ought in like manner to pronounce it to be white."* (Ibid, 181).

As a criterion on which good is distinguished from evil, the quality of feeling is taken, so it is considered that pleasant feelings are the evidence of the Spirit of God, and unpleasant feelings are the evidence of the spirit of the devil: *"The first is, that it is the property of God, and of every good Angel, to pour into the mind true spiritual joy, which they cause by taking away all that sadness arid disturbance of mind which the demon has thrown in whereas he, on the contrary, is accustomed by certain sophistical arguments bearing before them the appearance of truth [Autogragh, by bring ing forward apparent reasons, subtleties, and perpetual fallacies], to attack that joy found in the soul."* (Ibid, 157)

Since the first phase of spiritual exercises during the first week is based on causing unpleasant feelings, the rules for recognizing the spirits based on the pleasantness of emotion are learned only in the second week, and it is therefore emphasized: *"The eleventh (annotation) is, that for him who is exercising himself in the first week, it is expedient to be ignorant what he is to do in the next ; and to labour strenuously to obtain what he then seeks, as if he were about to find no good afterwards."* (Ibid, 6)

SUMMARY OF THE ANALYSIS OF THE SPIRITUAL EXERCISES OF IGNATIUS LOYOLA

Instead of reforming the motives of the heart, Loyola advocates the reform of feelings ie. mysticism, which represents an excitement of feelings, by which namely the awareness of the need for reforming the heart motives is suffocated. Since feelings depend on circumstances, a peace based on feelings can not be maintained without isolation from other people and without avoiding a human evil.

Unlike the experience of spiritual new birth which enables us to love people as they really are, Loyola, in his Spiritual Exercises advocates asceticism, which represents a separation from the world and thus avoidance of the stressful situations which would show that no internal reform of our heart motives has occurred.

Instead of obedience to God, Loyola demands obedience to the church, and instead of personal responsibility in understanding the truth, he elevates the authority of the priesthood and one's own feelings above personal conscience and reason.

In this way, he frees people from responsibility to think and decide on their own, thus disabling them to become aware of the above-described deception.

His philosophy and techniques by which he evokes the forces of human nature to religious zeal, Ignatius Loyola published in his work "Spiritual Exercises".

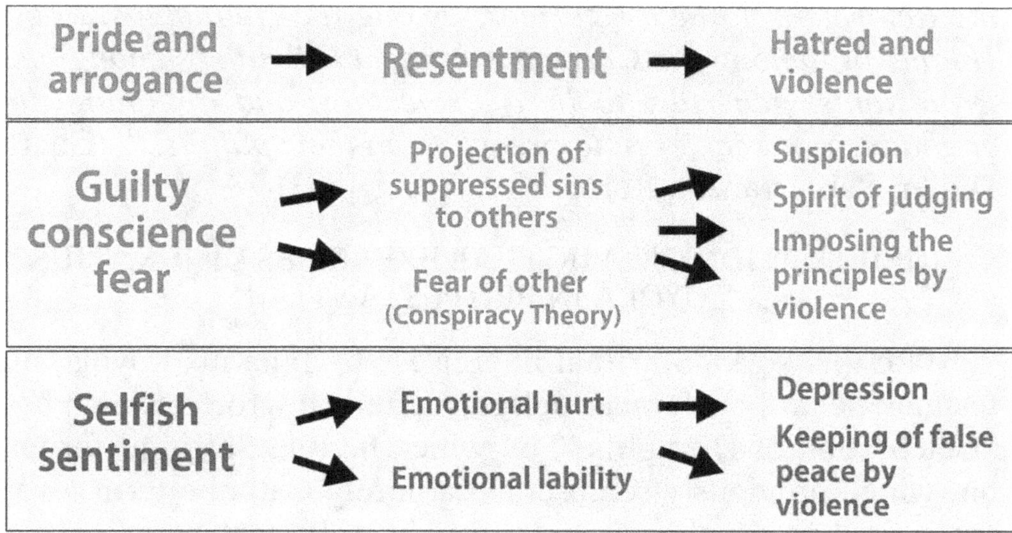

It should be kept in mind that Jesuit order is prone to violence by its very nature. The inclination of violence over conscience arises from the induced motives of human righteousness: guilt makes people suspicious and inclined to generate enemies from fear of conspiracy; pride makes people offensive and violent, and selfish sentiment - emotionally vulnerable and therefore prone to restrain in repressive way any criticism and discussion that would spoil her false peace.

The result of fear of the unclean conscience is a hypocritical restraint of a person's weaknesses of character in their expression, their projection to others through suspicion and judgements, and a tendency to impose these moral values on others by violence upon their conscience.

French writer and lawyer Etienne Pasquier (1529-1615) noticed and wrote about the Jesuits: *"Introduce this Order in our midst and, at the same time, you will introduce dissension, chaos and confusion"*. (H. Fulop-Miller: "Les Jesuites et le secret de leur puissance", Plon, Paris 1933, p.57)

Not a small number of times, the Jesuits were, because of their spirit of provocation of conflicts, expelled out of countries where they previously had free action. But their methods are not only aggressive, they are often very subtle. Their principle is: *"Among the Reformers, to be a reformer; among the Huguenots, to be a Huguenot; among the Calvinists, to be a Calvinist; among other Protestants, generally to be a Protestant, and obtaining their confidence, to seek even to preach from their pulpits...”* (Charles Didier, Subterranean Rome, New York, 1843)

INFILTRATION OF SPIRITUAL EXERCISES OF IGNATIUS LOYOLA IN PROTESTANTISM

With the work “Spiritual Exercises” by Ignatius Loyola, protestant Richard Foster was delighted, and he wrote his own book “Celebration of Discipline”, by which he, the Spiritual formation, which previously represented a purely Catholic term for the mentioned spiritual exercises, brought in Protestantism. The teaching of Richard Foster is worse than the teaching of Ignatius Loyola, for it states that the Law of God is abolished on the cross of Golgotha. Differently from the focus on arousing of fear of an unclean conscience, which is typical for traditional Catholicism, Richard Foster moves the focus on evoking of the selfish sentiment, which is a feature of the modern hedonistic western world and, and thus of the apostate Protestantism. Richard Foster cites the Russian Orthodox mystic Theophan the Recluse when he says, *“To pray is to descend with the mind into the heart, and there to stand before the face of the Lord, ever-present, all seeing, within you.”* (Richard Foster, Celebration of Discipline, 19) Theophan the Recluse states that “Jesus prayer”- “Lord Jesus Christ, Son of God, have mercy on me, a sinner” isn’t the best way of prayer, because *“emotion towards God”*, *“warmth of heart”* are more important than Jesus’ name *“on our tongue”*. According to him, *“prayer — is an act of heart”*, and *“thinking about God — is an act of mind”*. Such an understanding, promoted by the Spiritual formation, forms a distorted conscience, and instead of making a decision for God against his sinfulness, a man considers that he is not sincere in prayer because his sinful nature does not want God.

And in order to achieve that his sinful heart finally desires God, he distorts the idea of God, until it becomes so debased, that it ignites fanaticism and the longings of his human sinful nature as the power of religious zeal.

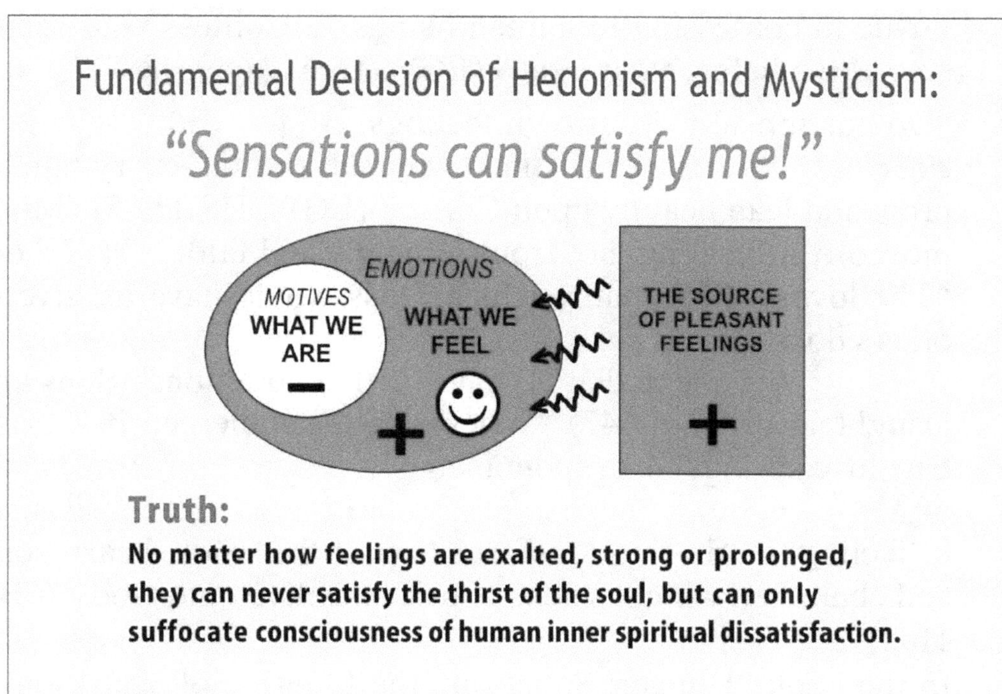

Through the book "Hunger: Satisfying the Longing of Your Soul", Jon Dybdahl introduces the Spiritual formation into the Adventist Church and advocates it as a dean of the "Walla Walla" University, and for a while he also lecturers it at Andrews University. This is especially intriguing, when we have in mind that Ellen G. White, as the light of truth in the Adventist Church, very precisely revealed in her extensive literary work every element of the deception of the Spiritual formation, when she wrote about the temptation of dwelling upon ourselves and our feelings, when she spoke of the manipulative power of the Catholic Mass, and when she explained the principles of false revival of the last days.

Her critique of the Spiritual formation could be most easily expressed by her warnings by which she promotes Christocentism and the rejection of any additional techniques in working out a communion with God:

"Bring nothing into your preaching to supplement Christ, the wisdom and power of God." (EGW, CET 247.1)

"I hope that none will obtain the idea that they are earning the favor of God by confession of sins or that there is special virtue in confessing to human beings. ... Confess your secret sins alone before your God." (EGW T5 647,649, 1889)

"Do not appeal to your own feelings. Do not think that sentimentalism is religion. Shake yourselves from every human prop, and lean heavily upon Christ." (EGW, HS 137.5) "Many moved from feeling, not from principle and faith ..." (1TT 64) "The love and sympathy which Jesus would have us give to others does not savor of sentimentalism, which is a snare to the soul; it is a love that is of heavenly extraction." (Sons and Daughters of God, 147) "When self is submerged in Christ, true love springs forth spontaneously. It is not an emotion or an impulse, but a decision of a sanctified will. It consists not in feeling, but in the transformation of the whole heart, soul, and character, which is dead to self and alive unto God." (6BC 1100)

In the book "Hunger: Satisfying the Longing of Your Soul " of Jon Dybdahl, we find the rhythmic repetition of prayer and the special significance of ambience and scent for the *"deeper experience of God,"* as if the communion with God depends on the feelings, and not on our belief in God and renunciation of sin.

Like Richard Foster, Jon Dybdahl also emphasizes the importance of the position of the body during prayer. In the work of Jon Dybdahl we can find techniques of confession, meditation ("reflection"), reliance on priests ("mentors"), rhythmic repetition of prayer as a kind of mantra, dealing with oneself and one's body (a kind of yoga), authenticity (sincerely following of one's Ego) and various other misconceptions which are the characteristics of modern Protestantism.

Similar perceptions are promoted by psychologist Julian Melgosa, who, like Jon Dybdahl, was dean of the "Walla Walla" University.

Dr. Julian Melgosa gives the wrong role to the confession of sins, leading the men to seek salvation in the very act of confession. In his book "Less Stress" in the chapter "Causes of Stress" he sees the cause of bad stressful reactions in the stress situation itself, and not in the separation of man from God. And then he advocates the deception that sins must first be confessed to the one to whom they have been committed, and only then to God: *"Christ taught his followers to reconcile with fellow humans before reconciliation with God."* And then, in order to justify this deception, Melgosa calls upon the verses that speak of the offering of the gift to God in His temple (Matthew 5:23), as if a man reconciles with God not behind the closed door of the personal communion with Him (Matthew 6: 6), but only when he goes to church to offer God a gift.

Of course, before offering a gift, a man should be reconciled with God and with his fellow men, but it is impossible for a man to sincerely reconcile with his neighbor, if he did not reconcile with God before, and receive from Him the forgiveness and love which he then shares with others. Julian Melgosa reveals the principle of the Spiritual formation - the searching for the salvation in everything except in God, even in those elements of relationships with other people that should be the natural result of a communion already realized with God, and not its foundation or cause.

As the author of biblical lesson for the first quarter of 2011, Julian Melgosa promotes the same deception as Jon Dybdahl through it, that the true love, which God gives us, is - emotion, and that our sense of life should be - enjoying in the emotion of love.

It is astonishing when Christian psychologists can not or do not want to understand the difference between the feeling of love that is the feature of human nature and the motive of true love that is exclusively the driving force of those people who are in communion with God.

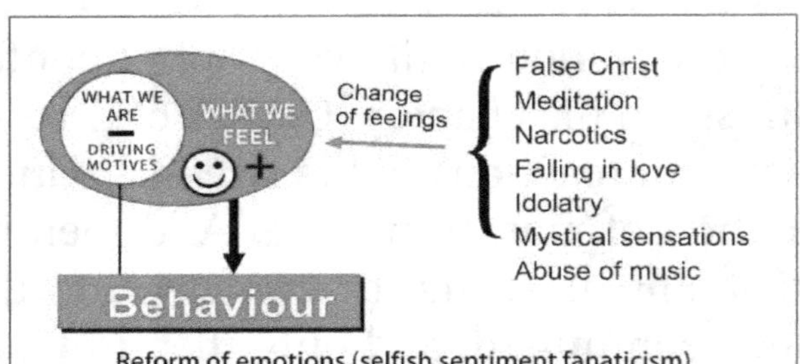

Reform of emotions (selfish sentiment fanaticism)

Reform of motives (real love)

It is true that the feeling of love itself can never satisfy the thirst of the soul because it is just a feeling. Feelings, no matter how exalted and powerful, are unable to replace the personal union of a man with God. Their abuse for the sake of satisfaction, constitutes a violation of the First Commandment, because then man puts them in a place of God.

Psychiatrist Torben Bergland, head of the Department of Health (TED Health Ministries director), promotes Spiritual formation through Health Clubs, advocating that the cure for addicts is to give them an emotion of love. His principle is that the opposite category of addiction is not sobriety but connection. By this, he leads the addicts to change one addiction with another addiction.

The misuse of the feelings for satisfaction represents the excitement of selfish motives of a sinful human nature and therefore belongs to the first phase of Ignatius Loyola's exercises. But as the person who is inebriating with feelings becomes hypersensitive to insults and vulnerable, has the need for the second phase of Ignatius Loyola exercises, which represent the system of techniques that removes the unpleasant symptoms of aroused bad motives from the first phase of the exercise. The need for the second phase, in order to avoid the vulnerability and offensiveness of the great Ego, will make the person receptive for the mistakes in the book "Boundaries".

The book "Boundaries" was written by two psychologists, Dr. Henry Cloud and Dr. John Townsend, whose names are on the list of accredited adherents of the Spiritual formation. Besides the emphasized egocentrism instead of Christcentrism, the authors of the "Boundaries" emphasize the deception by which many psychologists liberate their patients of their own responsibility, and that is the delusion that for their present mistakes and sins - their parents are guilty, guilty because they have caused them traumas even in their early childhood. Since the very teaching of the Spiritual formation is based, not on trusting in God, but on the reliance upon diverse techniques, the advocates of the Spiritual formation often praise contemporary psychology and consider that it has made a great contribution to the Spiritual formation itself.

The essential idea of the book "Boundaries" - that by the boundaries we can solve problems in our relationships with other people, was actually derived from Richard Foster's notion that a man must not only fall into a bondage to the Law in relation to God, but also that he can become a slave of the Law through relationship with other people. If a man has to restrain his repulsive tongue in relation to other people, isn't he in the bondage of the Law, asks Richard Foster. Accordingly, the authors of the book "Boundaries" argue that freedom implies the liberation of responsibility to love people as they are, simply by forming boundaries in relation with other people, the boundaries, that will prevent these people from hurting and humiliating our unconquered great Self. The authors of the "Boundaries", Dr. Henry Cloud and Dr. John Townsend, do not promote freedom when they speak of the victory of a man over his own sins, but they openly praise God for giving them freedom in Jesus which, according to them, represents freedom from the Law itself.

The deception of the Spiritual formation enters churches also through the unconverted psychologists. The aim of health and psychological seminars is that by their program they make people aware of their real spiritual condition and so awake their need for God. If those seminars are conducted improperly, they can produce the opposite effect - the suffocation of the need for God.

Take, for example, the decision of the General Conference of SDA to bring together a group of psychologists who will make an Adventist version of the 12-step program - "Twelve Step Recovery" for giving up the addiction.

The apparent intention was to use the popularity of the existing 12-step program to preach in its name the truth of the Gospel. But, since this responsibility is entrusted to psychologists, and not evangelists, they have opened the door of the church to the deceptions of Spiritual formation from within. *Instead of the 12-step program becoming a cover and a cause for promoting the truth of the Bible in the victory over vices, the Bible has become a cover and an excuse for promotion of deceptions of the Spiritual formation.* The Twelve Step Recovery program represents all deceptions of the Spiritual formation, leading a man to fortify his struggle against vice in dwelling upon himself, and not God.

TRAGIC CONSEQUENCES OF SPIRITUAL FORMATION

The consequences of the set of delusions represented by the Spiritual formation are catastrophic for the souls of those who adopt them, because they form unreasonable and immature persons from them. Unreasonable, because they do not distinguish the motive of true love from the motive of selfish sentiment, pride, and unclean conscience. Immature, because they are incapable of having feelings adequate to reality. In this state of spirit, they not only become unable to endure the persecution of the last days, but also they don't see why they would give the warning message of the fall of Babylon and the call for its leaving, when they themselves represent the teachings and techniques of Babylon.

Then, when the institutions of confession, mentor or group as intermediaries, mystical knowledge of God and the subtle justification by the deeds, are brought into a church which, by its doctrine, is indeed the pillar and fortress of truth, then every criticism of the poisonous wine of Babylon becomes devoid of meaning. For example, if *"the presence of another man makes God's presence more realistic"* (Dr M. Lukic, TSB) as is advocated by the bearers of Spiritual formation, then icons, statues and mediation of saints and priests also have their own justification, if reliance on *them "makes God's presence more realistic".* Enmity with essential deceptions of Catholic doctrine and modern apostate Protestantism cease when their deception is found in the Church of the Remnant. While the apologists of the Church have invested all forces to defend the question of Trinity, they have become blind before the delusion about God's character represented by the Spiritual formation, which is far more dangerous than the delusion about God's nature. While the apologists strain out a gnat, they swallow a camel. Yet, president of the General Conference of Seventh-day Adventist Church - Ted Wilson warned in his statement from July 2010:

> "Do not succumb to the mistaken idea, gaining support even in the Seventh-day Adventist Church, of accepting worship or evangelistic outreach methods merely because they are new and 'trendy.' We must be vigilant to test all things according the supreme authority of God's Word and the counsel with which we have been blessed in the writings of Ellen G. White. Don't reach out to movements or megachurch centers outside the Seventh-day Adventist Church which promise you spiritual success based on faulty theology. Stay away from non-Biblical spiritual disciplines or methods of Spiritual formation that are rooted in mysticism such as contemplative prayer, centering prayer, and the Emerging church movement in which they are promoted. Look within the Seventh-day Adventist Church to humble pastors, evangelists, Biblical scholars, leaders, and departmental directors who can provide evangelistic methods and programs that are based on solid Biblical principles and 'The Great Controversy Theme.' ... Guard against mystical beliefs and practices that are finding their way into the church through formats like Spiritual formation and the Emerging church... Stay away from mystical forms of prayer such a contemplative prayer, prayer labyrinths, repetitive prayer using one word or a certain phrase, or centering prayer that seem to

have become popular but lead to the occult since in many cases all thoughts are eliminated... Avoid the practice of inviting major spiritual speakers who are not Seventh- day Adventists to speak to church meetings, men's meetings, women's meetings, retreats, pastoral meetings, youth meetings, and large convocations... They probably have no concept of the great controversy theme... We need to be very proactive in requesting humble, Bible-centered Seventh-day Adventist speakers to instruct our church members in fully understanding God's great Biblical messages for this time.

Use Christ-centered, Bible-based worship and music practices in church services.... Don't go backwards into confusing pagan settings where music and worship become so focused on emotion and experience that you lose the central focus on the Word of God. All worship, however simple or complex, should do one thing and one thing only: lift up Christ and put down self. Worship methods that lift up performance and self should be replaced with a simple and sweet reflection of a Christ-centered, Biblical approach...

Resist worship styles and music that have more to do with self- centered entertainment than a humble worship of God...

We need to focus on worshipping God and not elevating self. Music should lift us to the throne room of heaven... If music sounds like it belongs to a hard rock concert or a nightclub, it should stay there." (Ted Wilson)

ANALYSIS OF THREE DECEPTIONS OF SPIRITUAL FORMATION

The Spiritual formation is characterized by three deceptions that are very popular in contemporary psychology, which provides symptomatic solutions to people who want only to remove the unpleasant consequences of sin from themselves (tension, nervousness, feeling of guilt, conflict with other people, etc.), but not give up sin which is the essential source of their problems. These three deceptions are: the confession of all sins to another person, the blaming of parents and other people for one's own sins and the inebriating with the emotion of being loved, by which the awareness of spiritual emptiness is suffocated. We will start from the most popular deception, the inebriating with feelings, which is the consequence of the wrong conception of the character of true love and the neglected importance of God's law.

INEBRIATING WITH EMOTION OF LOVE

Writer Jon Dybdahl leads people to seek God in order to satisfy their desire for pleasure:

"Our view of faith need not abandon the rational, but moves on to actually feel God's presence. That sense is something money can't buy. ... Setting the stage. ... I know one woman who creates her special setting by first opening the door to let God into the room before she begins to pray. Others use a special prayer rug or kneeling bench. Some may light a candle or dim the lights. Perhaps a memento of a special experience with God will help you establish a personal setting. Even special scents can help. ...

The specific aroma triggered in God's people a sense of His nearness. We must find all the ways we can to create in our lives places of "sweet fragrance" that elicit for us a sense of divine presence. When we enter such a place, we have already begun to pray, because we have reached out to God." (Jon Dybdahl, Hunger: Satisfying the Longing of Your Soul)

Is it possible, by evoking feelings, to force God to enter into the man's heart?

Is the emotion of love a remedy for the empty human heart?

Feelings that we feel are always adequate to some reality, either external or internal, and therefore, by dealing with them, we do not solve the problem, but we only eliminate the experience of the problem. If feelings of guilt, anxiety, psychical tension and nervousness reveal our inner spiritual state, a solution is not to turn to external sources of pleasant feelings and in this way suffocate the awareness of our internal problem.

Jesus blessed all who are aware of their need for God, and not those who managed to suffocate their need: *"The poor in spirit are blessed, for the kingdom of heaven is theirs. Those who mourn are blessed, for they will be comforted. ... Those who hunger and thirst for righteousness are blessed, for they will be filled."* (Matthew 5:3-6)

Evoked feelings present suffocating a man's need for God. Awareness of the sinfulness of the heart and the need for its reform disappears under such emotional rapture and the person is satisfied, not with the character of God who has heard him, but with himself and his own feelings by which he suffocated his need for God. He does not praise God's character, but his own feelings. Professor of the one Theological Seminary, advocates:

"God expects from his people's emotions ... God wants our emotions to swell, to mature, to expand, to fly together with His." (M. L. "God of the Hot Heart", 07/22/2017)

The Twelve Step Recovery program represents in step 11 dwelling upon ourselves and our feelings, and instead of God himself as an object of our reliance, the very act of prayer and meditation is presented to us:

"Meditation naturally brings together and centers the interaction of these different bodies with our spiritual body. Physically, meditation affects us in many wonderful ways. It increases the production and flow of endorphins that naturally calm and soothe our body. It lowers our blood pressure, helps to re-align our brain patterns and thought processes, and allows our body to begin healing itself. Emotionally, meditation helps to reduce the intensity and frequency of our resentments and fear, moving toward a more consistent feeling of caring, compassion and love. ... The first step in beginning of learning how to meditate is learning to relax our bodies, how to not listen to the "voices" of our mind and to practice connecting with our Higher Power and other human beings." (Journey to Wholeness - Twelve Step Recovery, step 11, page 44-45)

A LEAP OF ENDORPHINS AND DOPAMINE IN THE FIGHT AGAINST REASON AND CONSCIENCE

The 12 steps program "Journey to Wholeness" praises the endorphin leap during meditation, and it is known that endorphin is a neurotransmitter called "natural drug".

The feeling of alcohol-induced drunkenness is a direct consequence of the endorphin leap under the influence of alcohol. It is known that any behavior induced by a leap of endorphin is a temptation for addictive behavior.

Endorphin is a natural opiate which blocks the feeling of pain, but also, like dopamine, blocks an orbitofrontal cortex in the brain charged for responsible thinking and decision-making. Endorphin and dopamine have a vital function in activating other psychic abilities, which are certainly not adequate to those responsibilities and sobriety that are necessary for personal encounter with God. Sinful man is fighting against common sense, because reason makes him aware of the absurdity of sinful life and disturbs his conscience, calling him to reform. That's why a person uses different methods by which he increases the leap of dopamine and endorphin that block the orbitofrontal cortex that is in charge of self-assessment, judgment, and control.

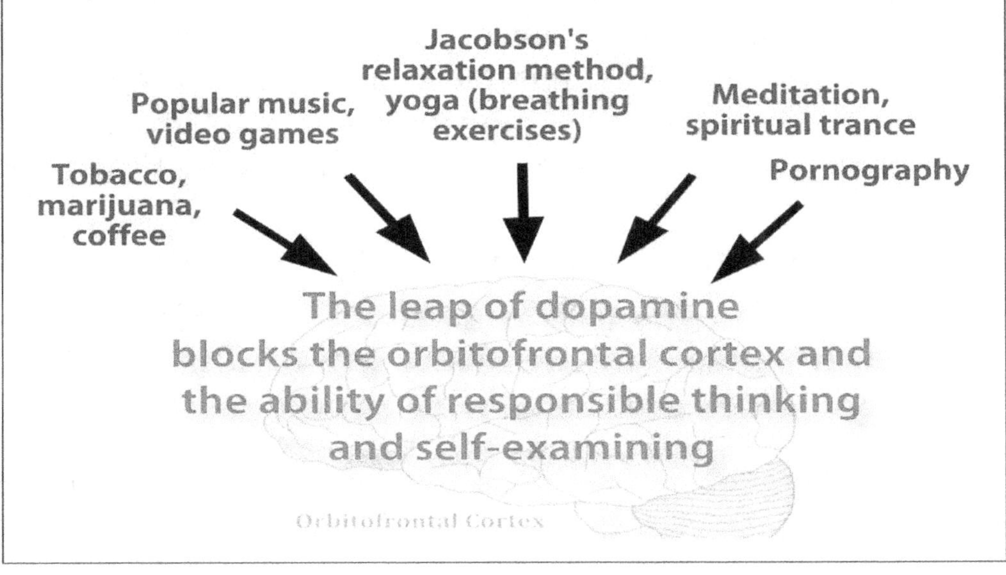

A leap of dopamine and endorphin is achieved by tobacco, narcotics, popular music, video games, meditation, yoga, breathing exercises and Jakobson's relaxation method. Reason and conscience are excluded and man loses consciousness about the problem.

Sugar in the blood also raises dopamine and endorphin, while a one-day week fast, when no food is eaten, results in a decrease in blood sugar, and therefore in a decline of dopamine and endorphin, and a leap of prolactin - a hormone of grief and care. That is why the fast can contribute a lot to our sobering and the awareness of sins of which we are otherwise unaware. During the true biblical fast, which represents a complete renunciation of food, many become disturbed because they become aware of their real spiritual state.

Let's notice the biblical examples where God calls people to take a fast and to fight against their sins, and they instead make a feast and create an atmosphere of euphoria with the same effects of modern meditation:

"On that day the Lord GOD of Hosts called for weeping, for wailing, ... But look: joy and gladness, butchering of cattle, slaughtering of sheep, eating of meat, and drinking of wine - "Let us eat and drink, for tomorrow we die!"" (Isaiah 22:12-13)

"Cleanse your hands, sinners, and purify your hearts, double-minded people! Be miserable and mourn and weep. Your laughter must change to mourning and your joy to sorrow. Humble yourselves before the Lord, and He will exalt you." (James 4:8-10)

"Sorrow is better than laughter: for by the sadness of the countenance the heart is made better." (Ecclesiastes 7:3)

The purpose of the fast is contrary to the purpose of meditation or any other false spiritual experience which, by evoked feelings, suffocates the awareness of a man for need for internal reform. Therefore, in a sound spiritual experience, the conception of Christian meditation would be most appropriately defined by the biblical term "Wrestling with God":

"In the womb he grasped his brother's heel, and as an adult he wrestled with God. Jacob struggled with the Angel and prevailed; he wept and sought His favor. He found him at Bethel, and there He spoke with him." (Hosea 12:3-4)

"I have seen God face to face, and my life is preserved." (Genesis 32:30)

In the book "Boundaries", we have an explanation of Jacob's wrestling with God, not as a conception of submitting of will to God, but as a conception of a wrestling that is an expression of Jacob's unconverted nature, because Jacob allegedly had an *"aggressive"* character (Boundaries, 53). We see an obvious attempt to turn a person away from the real encounter with God and to put other people on the throne of his heart. But let's look at the explanation of the conception of wrestling with God in Ellen G. White's writings:

"Those who are unwilling to deny self, to agonize before God, to pray long and earnestly for His blessing, will not obtain it. Wrestling with God—how few know what it is! How few have ever had their souls drawn out after God with intensity of desire until every power is on the stretch. When waves of despair which no language can express sweep over the suppliant, how few cling with unyielding faith to the promises of God." (EGW, GC 621.2)

"The warfare against self is the greatest battle that was ever fought. The yielding of self, surrendering all to the will of God, requires a struggle; but the soul must submit to God before it can be renewed in holiness." (EGW SC 44)

Of course, the most important thing is to know who we are praying to, lest we, due to the distorted perception of God's character, ask God to satisfy those sinful desires from which we need liberation, and not satisfaction. But knowing God in the Program of 12 steps does not in any way imply the knowledge of God's law that would rebuke the sinful motives of the human heart and thus relieve the person of the need for pleasure, but it states that everybody should believe in their personal interpretation of the God which they want to have. The consequence is that the participants of Program of 12 steps have such distorted conception of God and spiritual concepts, which Ellen G. White criticizes when she speaks of the deceit of fallen Christianity:

"Even in its present form, so far from being more worthy of toleration than formerly, it is really a more dangerous, because a more subtle, deception. While it formerly denounced Christ and the Bible, it now professes to accept both. But the Bible is interpreted in a manner that is pleasing to the unrenewed heart, while its solemn and vital truths are made of no effect. Love is dwelt upon as the chief attribute of God, but it is degraded to a weak sentimentalism, making little distinction between good and evil. God's justice, His denunciations of sin, the requirements of His holy law, are all kept out of sight. The people are taught to regard the Decalogue as a dead letter. Pleasing, bewitching fables captivate the senses and lead men to reject the Bible as the foundation of their faith. Christ is as verily denied as before; but Satan has so blinded the eyes of the people that the deception is not discerned." (EGW GC 558.1)

FOR A SELFISH HEART, EMOTION IS NOT A CURE, BUT A POISON

Exactly such conception about God is advocated by the psychiatrist Torben Bergland, president of the Health Department at the Division level. As part of the promotion of 12-step program, he advocates that a cure for the addicts is to give them an emotion of love. His principle is that the opposite category of addiction is not sobriety but connection. By this, he leads the addicts to replace addiction from opiates with addiction from emotion of love. Such an understanding is adequate to the temptation of contemporary Western hedonism, which is based precisely on emotional immaturity and the abuse of feelings for the sake of pleasure. God's cause among the white population of the West is threatened precisely because of such deception, because their sins are not rebuked, but they are wanted to be gained for the community by satisfying their unrebuked sins, which are proclaimed as natural human needs.

The person who nourishes his selfish human Ego with emotions, becomes emotionally too sensitive and vulnerable in time, and as the appetites of his Ego grow, they become unquenchable to such an extent that they keep a person in a constant state of depression, attached to a support group, which is trying to satisfy his need for feeling of being loved.

The misconception that the feeling of being loved is a cure for the soul of addicts of opiates is one of the key settings of the 12-step program. Perhaps this is the most clearly revealed by the views of the psychiatrist Torben Bergland. When he states that the root of each addiction is - emptiness, he does not see the fulfillment of that emptiness in building a communion of man with God, but in the closeness of man with another man and in a feeling caused by being loved: *"Acknowledging the emptiness or pain you are trying to manage through the addiction can be half the solution. The other half is getting connected with others, getting your needs covered by things that can truly fulfill, and by noting your victories, not your failures. ... Help yourself by helping others." (Torben Bergland, tedNEWS)*

He advocates that a quality emotional relationship is the basis of mental health, and, in fact, it is vice versa. In order for a person to have a good emotional relationship, he must first be mentally healthy, ie. he should be an emotionally mature person. Maturity, by definition, is putting our abilities in the proper function, in order to respond to the real needs of life, in contrast to immaturity, where the abilities are the tools of the satisfaction of the great Ego. Namely, the essence of emotional immaturity is in the abuse of the feelings for the sake of satisfaction.

An emotionally immature person is a selfish person, because he prefers the feelings that another person is causing him, rather than loving her personality. He does not realize that other people do not serve to fulfill his empty heart, or to cast away the feeling of loneliness from himself. Other people exist to be served, not for our personal satisfaction. Due to the lack of understanding of this fact and the distorted conception of the function of feelings, the participants of the 12 steps gradually become emotionally and socially immature personalities, hypersensitive, emotionally vulnerable and easily insulted, with very egocentric motives of socializing with other people.

The condition for any kind of maturity is the satisfied thirst of the soul in God. Without a personal communion with God, we will remain with an unsatisfied thirst of the soul and easily become addicted, either to narcotics, either to the support group, or to something else by which we substitute the absence of a real union with God. Christian writer Ellen G. White reveals such manifestations of immaturity of personality when she speaks of people in bondage of the need for socializing and entertainment (Messages to Young People 430), the bondage of emotional meetings (1T 412, 1864), emotional sermons (Manuscript 59, 1900), etc.

With aroused feelings of consolation and attention, a man of empty heart and unclean conscience only suffocates consciousness about his actual state and, therefore, the real need of his soul for God. Such a person, who is a slave of the inebriation with feelings, can only be helped by the reform of the inner heart motives, which will liberate her from the need for inebriating with the feeling of being loved, and not satisfy her need for feelings that are offered by the so-called support groups.

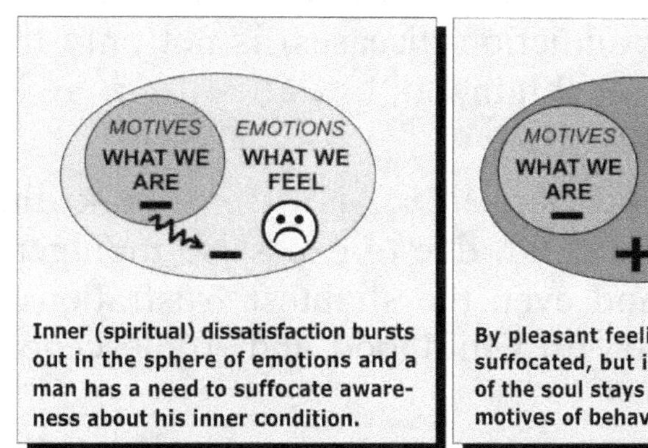

Inner (spiritual) dissatisfaction bursts out in the sphere of emotions and a man has a need to suffocate awareness about his inner condition.

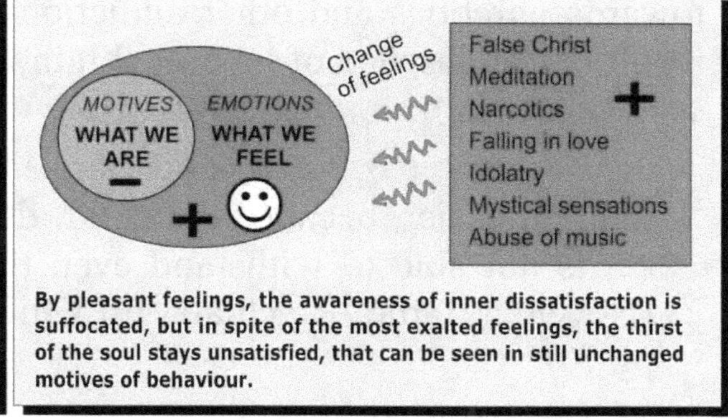

By pleasant feelings, the awareness of inner dissatisfaction is suffocated, but in spite of the most exalted feelings, the thirst of the soul stays unsatisfied, that can be seen in still unchanged motives of behaviour.

Such a reform of the essential motives of the heart can be fruit only of the encounter of a man with God, and not of the outwardly caused emotion of love. Lacking emotions of love during childhood, many Christian psychologists preach to their patients as an excuse for their current mental disorders and causes of addiction diseases. Patients feel great relief for their own conscience when they hear that their parents are guilty for their sins. In program of 12 steps Journey to Wholeness , there is an example of the experience of the program participant who, after confessing his secrets *"felt true acceptance and honest compassion for himself"* because *"it seemed less like something he did than something that happened to him."* (Journey to Wholeness - Twelve Step Recovery, step 5, p. 33) If a person is encouraged by other peoples's failures instead of their victories, what else does it reveal to us about the intentions of that person, than his intention to remain under the power of sin?! The conscience which calls for the confession of guilt before God because of surrendering to temptation, now finds its peace in the deception of the psychologists, and not in the liberating truth of the Gospel.

DISHONESTY OF MANY CHRISTIAN PSYCHOLOGISTS

Many Christian psychologists very unfairly omit the fact that the feeling of love, if it is overly provided during childhood, produces the same consequences as complete absence of love.

Fixation ie. attachment to the feelings that leads to the formation of an unquenchable need for inebriating (the tendency towards narcotics and other addiction diseases) is not only the result of the absence of love in childhood, but also of the excessive showing of love and attention:

"Excessive satisfaction and excessive frustrations make the fixation easier, because the child, due to excessive indulgence, is not able to withstand even the slightest frustrations." (Nevenka Tadić, Psychiatry in Childhood and Adolescence, pg 70)

"Insufficient or excessive gratification in any stage could lead to fixation in that stage and to the development of traits characteristic of that stage." (Spencer A. Rathus, Psychology: Concepts and Connections, pg 427)

"Alternatively, excessive gratification or frustration at any stage can lead to regression, which is a tendency to revert to a prior psychosexual level in the face of conflict or stress." (Irving B. Weiner, W. Edward Craighead, The Corsini Encyclopedia of Psychology, Volume 2, pg 529)

"Both excessive gratification and excessive frustration can shape the nature of adult character traits as well as neurotic adjustments." (E. Jerry Phares, Introduction to personality, pg 96)

"Psychopathology or mental health problems may also be caused by a fixation to any of these stages of development. Fixation may develop as a result of excessive frustration or excessive gratification." (Poul Rohleder, Critical Issues in Clinical and Health Psychology, pg 24)

Why is this truth - that pleasant feelings can produce the same unquenchable need for inebriating with feelings as well as frustration of child's need for love - hidden from people?

Because that fact would show all the senselessness of counsels of pseudo-Christian psychologists:

If the excessive provision of the feeling of love and attention spoiled a person at the time of her childhood, how could the same feeling of love and attention now heal her? Following their logic, people would conclude that a person, who was overly loved in her youth, now has a tendency towards inebriating, of which she would allegedly be liberated, by receiving the same feelings of being loved which has ruined her in her youth!

It would be too clear that the same feeling of love that spoiled the person, can not help her now. Such a person needs to be provided by true love, but at least through feelings, because she will misuse them, as she misuses them from childhood.

Do we have a biblical confirmation that a person who was denied at a young age in satisfying his needs, can not be healed later if his dreams are finally fulfilled?

The Bible reveals the whole tragedy of people who were denied in the satisfaction of their desires, and then one day, as adults, they finally succeeded in their desires:

"Under three things the earth quakes, And under four, it cannot bear up: Under a slave when he becomes king, And a fool when he is satisfied with food, under an unloved woman when she gets a husband, and a maidservant when she supplants her mistress." (Proverbs 30:21-23)

A person who reacted immaturely to poverty, becomes unquenchable greedy when offered as a solution an emotional satisfaction of her need. Likewise, a person who was not loved, reacts by a sinful nature in such a way that she is overwhelmed by the irrepressible need to inebriate with the feeling of being loved.

Although she became emotionally immature and addicted because she may have been frustrated in a real need for love in her youth, she can not now be helped by providing a feeling of being loved, because she abuses it for inebriating and suffocating the awareness of her spiritual emptiness. A person who is addicted will naturally abuse the feeling of closeness and feeling of being loved in order to inebriate with it in the same way she usually intoxicates with alcohol, narcotics, imagination, music and other opiates.

The true solution for a person who is an addict is not the reform of her feelings, but the reform of herself. She needs a reform of the motives of the heart, when through the communion with God she becomes free from selfish motives that prompt her to inebriate with feelings. This experience is called the experience of spiritual new birth. Hence, she can only be helped by repentance for the unquenchable selfish need for inebriating with feelings, by relying on God who changes the motives of heart, not feelings that need to remain adequate to the reality of life.

IS THE ESSENCE OF OUR PERSONALITY IN OUR WILL OR IN OUR EMOTIONS?

Is the essence of our personality in the emotions that govern us or in the will by which we govern ourselves and the world around us? If the essence of our personality were in our feelings, then we would not have our own personality, because the feelings depend on the circumstances. Let's pay attention to this misconception promoted in Saturday school lessons:

"Emotions are a vital part of the human personality. They can be powerful motivators, both for good and for evil." (Sabbath school lesson, December 25–31, 2011)

Likewise Julian Melgosa promotes:

"One could argue, justifiably, that emotions rule our lives to a much greater extent than reason does or ever could. Emotions are good; without them we'd barely be human. Robots might be able to function emotionlessly; we never could." (Dr. Julian Melgosa, "Jesus Wept": The Bible and Human Emotions)

Spiritual formation representatives, even if they were psychologists, show elemental ignorance of the human psyche, since they do not differentiate between the conception of feeling from the conception of driving motives. Feelings serve to feel by them, and not to distinguish good from evil by them (which is the role of reason), neither to decide by them (what is the role of the will), nor to be our initiator (which is the purpose of inner motives).

Emotions depend on circumstances, so that they are not a vital part of human personality. The essence of our personality is our will, which with the help of reason and conscience chooses the meaning of life through good or bad driving motives and thus determines our personality, and not our feelings, which are subject to change under various external and internal influences.

Without our personal will, reason and conscience, we would be like robots or animals!

That is why the Bible tradition presents emotions as the "kidneys" that "jump for joy", depending on the experience of reality, whereas the term "heart" denotes our essence (a essential part of our personality), which includes reason, will and chosen driving motives. In Webster's dictionary we read about the meaning of the kidneys (reins): "Webster: Definition of REINS 1 a : kidneys b : the region of the kidneys : loins 2 : the seat of the feelings or passions". And in Easton's Bible Dictionary we read about meaning of the heart: "The heart is the "home of the personal life," and hence a man is designated, according to his heart, wise (1 Kings 3:12, etc.), pure (Ps. 24:4; Matt. 5:8, etc.), upright and righteous (Gen. 20:5, 6; Ps. 11:2; 78:72), pious and good (Luke 8:15), etc. ... The heart is also the seat of the conscience (Rom. 2:15).

It is naturally wicked (Gen. 8:21), and hence it contaminates the whole life and character (Matt. 12:34; 15:18; comp. Eccl. 8:11; Ps. 73:7)." In the plan of salvation, God changes essential motives of our heart (ourselves), not our feelings:

"Then the Spirit of the LORD will come upon you mightily, and you shall prophesy with them and be changed into another man." (1 Samuel 10:6)

"But this is the covenant which I will make with the house of Israel after those days," declares the LORD, "I will put My law within them and on their heart I will write it; and I will be their God, and they shall be My people." (Jeremiah 31:33)

"I will give you a new heart and put a new spirit within you; I will take the heart of stone from your body and give you a heart of flesh. I will put my spirit in to you and make you conform to my statutes, keep my laws and live by them." (Ezekiel 36:26-27)

A NEW BIRTH IS A CHANGE OF HEART MOTIVES, NOT EMOTIONS

Let's look the comment of Ellen G. White for the term "new heart" on this verse:

"Many who speak to others of the need of a new heart do not themselves know what is meant by these words. The youth especially stumble over this phrase, "a new heart." They do not know what it means. They look for a special change to take place in their feelings. This they term conversion. Over this error thousands have stumbled to ruin, not understanding the expression, "Ye must be born again."

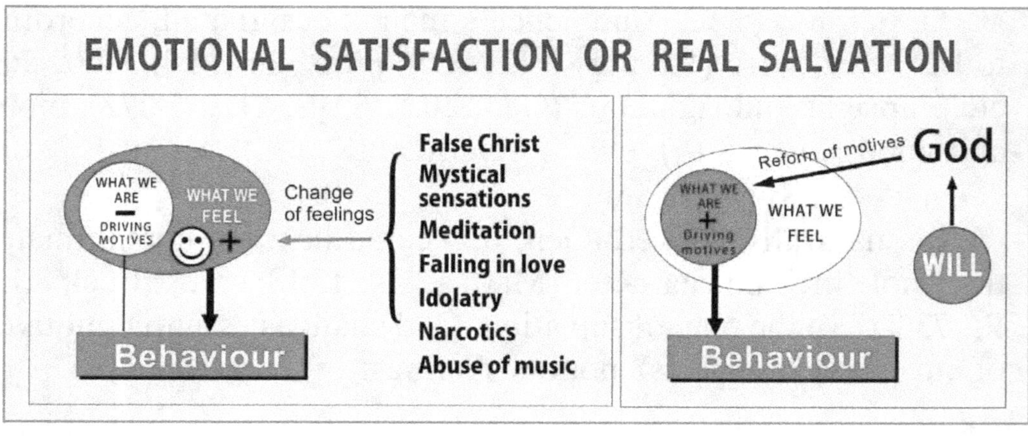

Satan leads people to think that because they have felt a rapture of feeling they are converted. But their experience does not change. Their actions are the same as before. Their lives show no good fruit. They pray often and long, and are constantly referring to the feelings they had at such and such a time. But they do not live the new life. They are deceived. Their experience goes no deeper than feeling. They build upon the sand, and when adverse winds come their house is swept away." (EGW MYP 71)

OUR FEELINGS SHOULD BE ADEQUATE TO REALITY

Unlike our motives that depend on our communion with God, our feelings depend on circumstances, and therefore they can not be the criterion of our spirit. They need to remain adequate to life's reality.

There is nothing wrong with having feelings which are in accordance with actual reality, because such feelings direct us to those activities which provide answers addressing real needs of life. It is normal that gain, beauty and goodness provoke appropriate feelings of joy.

However, it is up to us, to either misuse those pleasant feelings for our own satisfaction, which makes us selfish, or to be grateful for such feelings. If we foster a selfish attitude towards the source of our pleasant feelings, we pave the way for our depressive reaction which will occur the day our selfish attitude is thwarted. Thus, the mature reaction to the source of our pleasant emotions is the spirit of gratitude.

Mind	Emotions	Motives (bad or good)
Goodness, justice, gain, gift	Joy	Selfishness or gratitude
Danger	Fear	Cowardice or courage
Injustice	Anger	Hatred or meekness
Loss	Sadness	Worry or care

Similarly, it is normal to feel fear when we are facing danger. However, it is up to us whether we want to be cowards, or whether we want to be brave. If we act as cowards, we remain cowards although the danger has passed, but if we respond courageously, we remain courageous even after the challenge passes. Likewise, it is quite normal that injustice prompts in us adequate feeling of anger. However, it is up to us whether we respond to such injustice with hatred, or meekness. If we respond with hatred, hatred remains within us even when the external temptations are gone, but if we respond with meekness and forgiveness, we retain the built character of peace even after the source of injustice is removed. Moreover, it is quite normal that trouble, failure, or loss of loved ones, causes a corresponding feeling of sadness.

However, it is up to us whether we respond to such troubles with anxiety, or concern, and whether we respond to the loss of loved ones by falling into depression, or maintain reasonable equanimity.

IF THE THIRST OF OUR SOUL IS SATISFIED IN GOD, IT IS NOT MORE IMPORTANT TO US HOW WE FEEL

From our communion with God depend our driving motives and they determine the correct or incorrect function of our feelings. If the thirst of the soul is not satisfied in God, man will naturally begin to abuse feelings by inebriating with them. And if he is satisfied in God, he will be relieved of how he feels. In Ellen G. White's works we find a great light that unmasks the abuse of feelings:

"Do not exalt your feelings, and be swayed by them, whether they be good, bad, sad, or joyful. ... The soul's supply of nutrition is in Jesus Christ. A legal religion will always be a troublesome guest, and it is a deception to imagine that there is such a thing as natural religion that is acceptable to God. The religion of Christ teaches its possessor self-distrust, but at the same time enables him to grasp the hand of Christ firmly, and still more firmly, as temptations press upon the soul." (ST Dec. 3, 1894, par. 2)

"We are not to make our feelings a test by which to discern whether we are in or out of favor with God, whether they be what we consider encouraging or not. As soon as one begins to contemplate his feelings, he is on dangerous ground." (Signs of the Times, December 3, 1894. PH048 31)

"It is not wise to look to ourselves and study our emotions. If we do this, the enemy will present difficulties and temptations that weaken faith and destroy courage. Closely to study our emotions and give way to our feelings is to entertain doubt and entangle ourselves in perplexity. We are to look away from self to Jesus. (MH249, 1905)

"Many precious souls, earnestly desiring to be Christians, are yet stumbling in darkness, waiting for their feelings to be powerfully exercised. They look for a special change to take place in their feelings. They expect some irresistible force, over which they have no control, to overpower them. They overlook the fact that the believer in Christ is to work out his salvation with fear and trembling." (Ms55-1910)

"Selfishness is the strongest and most general of human impulses, the struggle of the soul between sympathy and covetousness is an unequal contest; for while selfishness is the strongest passion, love and benevolence are too often the weakest, and as a rule the evil gains the victory. Therefore in our labors and gifts for God's cause, it is unsafe to be controlled by feeling or impulse. To give or to labor when our sympathies are moved, and to withhold our gifts or service when the emotions are not stirred, is an unwise and dangerous course. If we are controlled by impulse or mere human sympathy, then a few instances where our efforts for others are repaid with ingratitude, or where our gifts are abused or squandered, will be sufficient to freeze up the springs of beneficence." (RH December 7, 1886, par. 5)

"The love of Christ in the heart is what is needed. Self is in need of being crucified. When self is submerged in Christ, true love springs forth spontaneously. It is not an emotion or an impulse, but a decision of a sanctified will. It consists not in feeling, but in the transformation of the whole heart, soul, and character, which is dead to self and alive unto God. Our Lord and Saviour asks us to give ourselves to Him. Surrendering self to God is all He requires, giving ourselves to Him to be employed as He sees fit. Until we come to this point of surrender, we shall not work happily, usefully, or successfully anywhere" (Letter 97, 1898). {6BC 1100.9}

SEARCHING FOR THE SALVATION IN THE CONFESSION TO ANOTHER PERSON

Instead of confessing his sin to the person he has offended in order to correct relationships with others, a man is said to confess all the sins of his life to the chosen person, only to psychologically compensate for the real relief that he would have already received from God, if he sincerely repented for his sins. Such confession contains three elements of psychological satisfaction A) through psychic emptying, B) through getting used to his sin and through benumbing of the conscience, and C) through throwing the guilt for sins on others - external factors that are supposedly responsible for sin, as when Adam accuses Eve of his sin, and Eve - snake.

One preacher, a doctor of theology, who promotes the program of 12 steps, during the explanation of step no. 5 asks the question and then he answers:

"Why is not it enough to confess to ourselves and to confess to God? The answer to this question is because without confession to another man, there will be no healing. ... And nothing will happen when it comes to recovery, when the depth inside of should be healed, as long as we do not confess to the other person about who we are, to the end ... Personal prayer does not go beyond the ceiling. " (M. Lukic, Explanation of Step 5)

The purpose of confession to another person, according to the 12 steps Program, is to achieve *"freedom from the negative emotions associated with secret sins. ... True peace comes when we have not omitted any details, no matter how embarrassing we think they may be."* (Journey to Wholeness - Twelve Step Recovery, step 5, page 38, 43) That confession to another person benumbs a conscience, clearly reveals the very acknowledgment of preacher, the promoter of the 12 steps program:

"My experience is that when I once said my secret, the next time I said it much easier in front of a larger group of people. And then, next time, it was quite normal. I did not even consi-

der it a confession. That's me. Until at the end ... I no longer felt a shame because I am such." (M. Lukic, Explanation of Step 5)

It is interesting that the same person, who believes that by the time he ceases to feel shame due to confession of sin, declares that the feeling of shame is keeping him from sinning, and that without this shame there is no other motive out of which he would take responsibility for his actions:

"As long as someone else does not know about my problem ... I have no responsibility, simply. As long as I am alone with my own evil and trying to confess it to God alone, everything stays in darkness. But in the presence of other person, everything begins to come out. So, this vice wants to remain secret. It wants to be in the dark. It despises the light. ... When we tell God in secret or to ourselves, there is always an option to go back, there is this retreat, but when we tell the other ... then there is already a witness. No longer can any of the defense mechanisms to work." (M.L. Explanation of Step 5)

It is interesting that Ignatius Loyola, in his Spiritual Exercises, also advocates the confession of sin to another person as a protection against the repetition of that sin:

"In the same way, the devil studiously endeavours, that the soul which he desires to circumvent and ruin, should keep his deceitful suggestions secret; [Autograph, when the enemy of human nature suggests to a just soul his deceits and persuasions, he wishes and desires that they may be received and kept in secret;] but is in the highest degree displeased, and most grievously tormented, if his attempts be made known to any one, either hearing confession, or being a spiritual man [the Autograph adds : who may know his deceits and malice] ; because he understands that, such being the case, he altogether fails in them." (The Spiritual Exercises of St. Ignatius of Loyola, 156)

But it is a mistake to believe that our confession will save us from sin. First, because by the act of frequent confession of sin we benumb our conscience. Second, because the actual victory over sin can not be a consequence of the transfer of our responsibility to someone who, through guilt or embarrassment, only prevents us from manifesting sin.

Several scientific studies have shown that confession only

gives us psychological satisfaction (which normally is not necessary to the one who really repented for his sin), and that its trainees are worse than those who didn't go to any psychological treatment. A study published in the American Psychiatric Journal of 1967 showed that participants in Anonymous Alcoholics treatment had a higher rate of return to criminal acts than a non-treatment group. Similarly, the statistics of criminal psychopaths who return after treatment to their offenses (Rice, Harris, & Cormier, 1992) reveal that those who go to the treatment of mutual confession (Social Therapy Unit) are worse than a control group that didn't go for a treatment (77% to 55%).

Promoters of Spiritual formation often refer to the experience of emotional relaxation when they confess their sins and traumas from the past to others.

Many people think that it makes sense to recall the childhood traumas, in order to become aware of our defensive mechanisms, which are the consequence of our previous woundedness or insultedness.

However, when a man truly repents for his sins, these mechanisms lose strength, because such a man in doesn't have in his heart the sinful motives (as a strength of these mechanisms), so he can not even remember events with that same sinful spirit that previously led him to a sinful reaction.

For example, if by some kind of real injustice our arrogant Ego was hurt, so we became filled with hatred, now, after the conversion of our heart, we no longer have an arrogant Ego, neither offensiveness, nor hatred in the heart, so that same or similar event would cause the same reactions. If by thwarting of the real need for love we were emotionally wounded and fell into an insatiable (selfish) need for a feeling of being loved, now, when we are filled with God's love, we do not have anymore selfishness or emotional vulnerability, that the same stress could hurt us and produce depression.

If we really died to self, and if on the throne of our heart is Jesus Christ, then His Spirit is a spontaneous reaction to the same stressful situation, and it is the spirit of meekness, humility, selflessness and gratitude. The same stressful situation that provoked sin, now provokes the spirit of love.

If we, however, still cherish an unburied great Ego, so we can not endure the troubles, then we should confess to Jesus our great Ego, and not to excuse it by calling upon circumstances. A false religious belief does not reprimand sin at the root, so since we keep sin and its destructive reactions, we seek an excuse for our reactions in circumstances.

If somebody offends our pride or hurts our selfishness, we have the need to outflow our inner dissatisfaction through insultedness and hatred, or woundedness and depression. In psychical discharging, we can be also helped by easily retelling this event to others. As a psychically tense person sincerely feels relieved after watching a boxing match or through music with a expressed rhythm, so relieved is a person who has discovered his internal urges to another person through confession.

But the very psychical discharging, since it represents a kind of expression of sin, represents the development of that sin, and the very method of psychical discharging represents a kind of dependence. Instead of psychical discharging, the real solution is repentance for those sins of our great Ego, because of which we reacted immaturely to psychical wounding.

If we really genuinely repented for pride or selfishness, we will also have difficulty in the very act of recalling our insultedness or woundedness, because we will not have anymore motives in ourselves, by which we could sincerely experience this insultednesss or woundedness. The meek and unselfish spirit endures trouble with love, either in reality, or in recall. Relieved from spiritual dissatisfaction, filled with God's love, we are no longer psychically tense, so we do not have the need to psychically discharge. But if we kept the bad motives of the heart in ourselves, we will have the need to recall the problems, in order to psychically discharge through its expression.

Ellen G. White talks about recalling the past events that have wounded our soul, as a very detrimental way of seeking relief. She critically writes about the temptation of her husband, James White, who was constantly returning to the injustices inflicted by his brothers in the past:

> "But although the wrong was healed in the sight of God, yet he sometimes in his own mind probed that wound, and by referring to the past he suffered it to fester and make him unhappy." (EGW 1T 613.3)

> "I saw that my husband should not dwell upon the painful facts in our experience. Neither should he write his grievances, but keep as far from them as he can. The Lord will heal the wounds of the past if he will turn his attention away from them." (3T 98.2)

> "The remembrance of the unpleasant past only saddens the present, and he lives over again the unpleasant portion of his life's history. In so doing he is clinging to the darkness and is pressing the thorn deeper into his spirit. This is my husband's infirmity, and it is displeasing to God. This brings darkness and not light. He may feel apparent relief for the time in expressing his feelings; but it only makes more acute the sense of how great his sufferings and trials have been, until the whole becomes magnified in his imagination, and the errors of his brethren, who have aided in bringing these trials upon him, look so grievous that their wrongs seem to him past endurance." (3T 97.1)

> "Instead of bemoaning your weakness and talking unbelief and feeling that you are hardly used, begin to sing. Talk of the mercy and love of God. To all who labor and are heavy laden Christ gives the invitation, "Come unto Me, ... and I will give

you rest. Take My yoke upon you, and learn of Me; for I am meek and lowly in heart, and ye shall find rest unto your souls. For My yoke is easy, and My burden is light" [Matthew 11:28-30]. This is the lesson that Christ desires you to learn, and in learning it you will find rest." (EGW TSB 50.3)

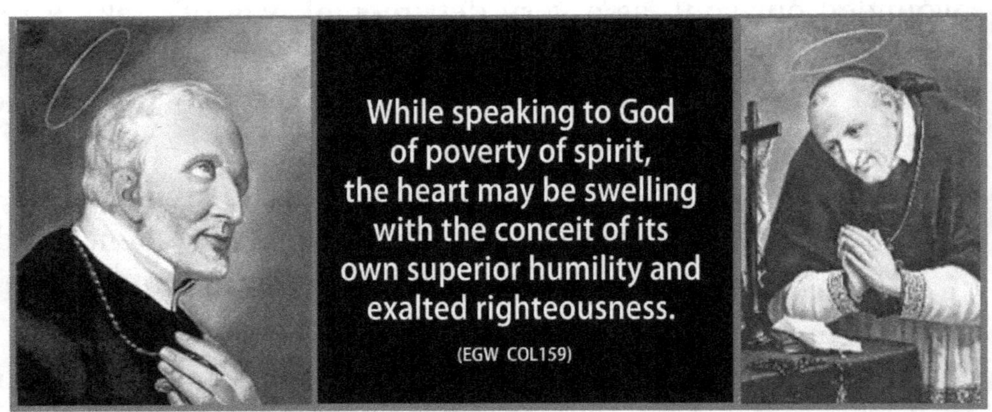

"Do not dwell upon the hardships of the Christian life. Do not talk of your trials; for if you do, you will become more and more inclined to complain of God. Talk of the love of Christ, bringing it into your heart and life." (EGW Letter 72, 1903)

"Every one needs a practical experience in trusting God for himself. Let no man become your confessor; open the heart to God; tell Him every secret of the soul. Bring to Him your difficulties, small and great, and He will show you a way out of them all. He alone can know how to give the very help you need." (EGW GW 418.3)

Advocates of the Spiritual formation have a wrong idea of the notion of humility. In humility they do not see a natural element of true love, which is the fruit of new birth, but they see a forced act of deliberate humiliation. However, being humiliated and being humble is not the same.

Even the confession of sin to God, if it is not the fruit of dwelling upon Jesus, but of dwelling upon ourselves, gets the wrong function and feeds our self-righteous Self:

"No man can of himself understand his errors. "The heart is deceitful above all things, and desperately wicked; who can know it?" (Jeremiah 17:9.) The lips may express a poverty of soul that the heart does not acknowledge. While speaking to God of poverty of spirit, the heart may be swelling with the conceit of its own superior humility and exalted righteousness.

In one way only can a true knowledge of self be obtained. We must behold Christ.

It is ignorance of Him that makes men so uplifted in their own righteousness.

When we contemplate His purity and excellence, we shall see our own weakness and poverty and defects as they really are. We shall see ourselves lost and hopeless, clad in garments of self-righteousness, like every other sinner." (EGW COL.159)

AWARENESS OF OTHER PEOPLE'S SINS AS A FOOD FOR ONE'S OWN UNCLEAN CONSCIENCE

People who have unconquered sins which they sincerely long to conquer, naturally long for the encouragement which they find in the experience of others who have conquered these same sins. But if they do not intend to reject their sins, they long for the experience of others' failure in order to justify their own failure. In 12-step program "Journey to Wholeness" we see a source of comfort and peace which mentor (sponsor) gives to the confessor by admitting that he himself did the same sins:

"One Fellow Traveler put it like this, 'My sponsor gave me a lot of feedback and never once criticized. He kept sazing, 'you too?' What that meant was that he had done a lot of the same things I had done! When I finished he said to me, "Well John, everything you shared I have heard before. You shared nothing I haven't heard before from my other sponsees." It was a burden carrying all the resentment, guilt and fear. Jerry was my sponsor, but I know people who have used Priests, Rabbis. Mullahs, counselors, etc." (Journey to Wholeness - Twelve Step Recovery, step 5, page 35)

If a person is encouraged by the failure of other people instead of their victories, what else it reveals about the intentions of that person but that he wants to remain under the power of sin?!

As they replaced the authority of Christ with their Self, and the appeals of the Holy Spirit with the desires of their sinful heart, these people show a pronounced inclination to proclaim every holiness of right life as acting and hypocrisy, because they interpret other people's actions through the motives of their own sinful heart. Had they themselves experienced the victory over their own temptations, they would also in others' experiences recognize the victory. And as they do not have this experience themselves, they want to deceive their conscience with the idea that victory is not possible, and to devalue every role model that invites them to such a victory.

What is the easiest way for a person to devalue an exalted reprimand for his own conscience?

By interpreting the exalted acts through the motives of his own unrenewed heart!

Mechanism of projection, when the acts of the holy biblical people are interpreted through the corrupt motives of one's own heart, we find among the representatives of the Spiritual formation.

For example, in the book "Boundaries", we have an explanation of Jacob's wrestling with God, not as a conception of submitting of will to God, but as a conception of a wrestling that is an expression of Jacob's unconverted nature, because Jacob allegedly had an *"aggressive"* character (Boundaries, 53).

While the open critics of Christianity often project to the biblical men a sinful character in order to have an excuse to reject the Bible as it supposedly represents and promotes evil, many Christians also make the same projection of sins in order to justify the same sins among themselves by wrong interpretation of the Scriptures.

Instead of achieving peace by harmonizing their life with sublime criteria that require the reform of their sinful hearts, they accomplish peace of their conscience by devaluing and debasing the exalted requirements of the Scriptures, until they become so low, that they can fulfill them with the power of their own sinful nature. In order to prevent persecution and calm the consciences of their listeners, modern-day Protestant preachers often openly emphasize how they cannot conquer their sins and how Jesus gave them freedom, not from lawlessness, but from the law itself. They thus gain authority among their listeners, because they provide them with a calming of their conscience that calls them on reform. The unconverted human heart, instead of looking beyond itself, through the revelation of God's character that will make him aware of the need for internal reform, has the need to look beneath itself, to find in the sins of others an excuse for its own sins.

One commentator of the 12-step program noted:

"The more miserable company they can help generate and surround themselves with in the fellowship, the more validated they feel living with their own wretchedness and preserving the unwillingness to face the truth about themselves that is necessary to awaken and recover.

It's exactly like thieves hanging out with thieves, or cannibals living in a community of other cannibals – no matter how low they sink, there's always everyone else in the same boat to justify a miserable existence." (Daniel J. Schwarzhoff, recoveredalcoholic.blogspot.com)

The advocates of the Spiritual formation desperately want to portray that a victory over sin is not possible, and therefore every supernatural example of the victory over sin they want to undervalue by the claim that it is a hypocrisy or a legalism, thus projecting the unconscious principles of their own vain spiritual struggle. They behave just as The Wisdom of Solomon describes the conduct of the wicked towards the righteous:

"Therefore let us lie in wait for the righteous; because he is not for our turn, and he is clean contrary to our doings: he upbraideth us with our offending the law, and objecteth to our infamy the transgressings of our education. He professeth to have the knowledge of God: and he calleth himself the child of the Lord. He was made to reprove our thoughts. He is grievous unto us even to behold: for his life is not like other men's, his ways are of another fashion. We are esteemed of him as counterfeits: he abstaineth from our ways as from filthiness: he pronounceth the end of the just to be blessed, and maketh his boast that God is his father. ... Let us examine him with despitefulness and torture, that we may know his meekness, and prove his patience." (The Wisdom of Solomon 2:12-19, Brenton Septuagint Translation)

Unclean conscience is the driving force that stands behind the persecution of anyone who upsets the unclean conscience.

In one class of one high school, all students were addicted to tobacco except for one single student. The rest of the students contininually put pressure on him to take a cigarette and to smoke. But unsuccessfully. One day, they physically surrounded him and threatened to take a smoke. As he did not consent, they disfigured his face with a burning cigarette. **People of unclean conscience can be very aggressive and violent towards the one who is a rebuke for their conscience.**

Let us remember the reason why Cain killed Abel:

"And for what reason did he slay him? Because his deeds were evil, and his brother's were righteous. Do not be surprised, brethren, if the world hates you." (1 John 3:12-13)

If our life is truly righteous, people will not speak positively about us. Jesus warns that our popularity among people is a sign that something is wrong with us:

"Woe to you when all men speak well of you, for their fathers used to treat the false prophets in the same way." (Luke 6:26)

If by stories that are pleasing to the carnal heart and by liberal life we are calming the conscience of others, people will talk about us well, which means that we are playing the role of ancient false prophets. But if we preach the truth that is the answer to the temptations that people have, their conscience will be moved to struggle, either against their own sins, or against us, because we have disturbed their spirit by sending them a call for reform.

The spirit of persecution follows every preaching of truth that demands renunciation, because those who do not war with themselves and their sins, war against those who have reprimanded them for their sins.

Some advocates of public confession believe that it is good for preachers to present themselves as sinners in the eyes of others, speaking that they should not look like Catholic saints, and that confession is a way to fight against their own cult among believers and against the tendency of believers to rely on them instead of on God. However, an open confession of their sins will just gain popularity among others, namely among those who in the sins of preachers will find an excuse for their own iniquities. People who truly live sacred life are not popular, because they represent a reproach for the conscience of the unrepentant. The prophet Elijah certainly did not have a cult and was not popular among the people.

There is a difference between the role model which makes a person aware of the need for his own reform, and the idol that by provoked feelings stifles that awareness.

Catholic saints are not role models which, by their appearance, reproach the sins of others, but they are mute and immobile idols unable to reproach the sins of the heart. They provide the masses of believers with the same psychological consolation as the support groups. The support groups can not reprimand sin, but with their advices and iniciated emotions they calm the conscience and suffocate the need of a human heart for internal reform.

Why is it bad to see in other the holy man, the righteous one, who successfully overcomes the daily temptations?

We will hear the answer: *"Because a man then feels sinful and weak!"*

But does not a person already feel sinful and weak in the light of God's face?

If our concept of God is right, as we look at Christ we will feel like the most sinful people in the world. But that does not mean that we will then live sinfully. The awareness of our sinfulness will then keep us glued to Christ. In Him we will find the answer to every need of our soul for forgiveness, heart reform and healing. By keeping the awareness of our own sinfulness, we will no longer rely on our own nature, and therefore it will no longer have power over us, as long as we rely on the power that is above us and which comes from God.

Who relies on God, he receives from God the power to live properly, as long as he does not rely on himself. But a person who is not in peace with God, he, because of the unclean conscience, has a strong need to feel that he is righteous, and that is why he is disturbed by every example of righteousness that is above him, as it results in feeling of his sinfulness. So, the fact that some people are bothered and not rejoiced when they see righteousness in others, reveals their problem with their own conscience.

In order to stifle the voice of conscience, people have a need to devalue every exalted pattern, and to lower the attention of their mind from the sublime Christ's example to the example of other people's sinning.

When, at the end of the nineteenth century, decadence in the Protestant nations grew to a such extent that the Holy Scripture was no longer the authority of life, it was no longer modern to speak of oneself as sinful. As soon as the spirit of the famous Protestant self-criticism was dead, racism arose and the need for a yellow press. Many Enlightenment journals, who have so far rebuked the sins of the people, have transformed themselves into a gossip press. The spirit of slandering and gossiping has risen. Taverns and pubs, which were places for self-critical discussion of life issues, turned into the places of entertainment. Friendly criticism began to be considered impolite, the notions of sin and guilt were expelled from everyday jargon and replaced by their euphemisms. Such a spirit imbued the apostate Protestantism as well as the newly emerging atheism. In the darkness of others' sins, people feel more righteous than in the light of God's face.

The same effect of deceiving one's own conscience is achieved through the public confession of personal sins, whether it is heard by the enemies of the Gospel, or by the alleged friends of the Gospel, to whom the awareness of the sins of other people, and especially of preachers give an excuse to repeat this sin when they are tempted.

How important is for the preacher of the Gospel to be a role model and reprimand for sins to others, and how harmful is the public confession of sins from the preachers themselves, explains Ellen G. White with the following words:

"Some who profess to be spokesmen for God are in their daily life denying the faith. They present to the people important truths; but who are impressed by these truths? who are convicted of sin? The hearers know that those who are preaching today will tomorrow be the first to join in pleasure, mirth, and frivolity. Their influence out of the pulpit soothes the conscience of the impenitent and causes the ministry to be despised. They are themselves asleep upon the Worldliness in the Church very verge of the eternal world. The blood of souls is upon their garments." (EGW 5T, 190)

"I have been shown that many, many confessions should never be spoken in the hearing of mortals; for the result is that which the limited judgment of finite beings does not anticipate. Seeds of evil are scattered in the minds and hearts of those who hear, and when they are under temptation, these seeds will spring up and bear fruit, and the same sad experience will be repeated. For, think the tempted ones, these sins cannot be so very grievous; for did not those who have made confession, Christians of long standing, do these very things?

Thus the open confession in the church of these secret sins will prove a savor of death rather than of life. ... I hope that none will obtain the idea that they are earning the favor of God by confession of sins or that there is special virtue in confessing to human beings. ... Confess your secret sins alone before your God. ... Your fellow men cannot absolve you from sin or cleanse you from iniquity. Jesus is the only One who can give you peace." (EGW T5 647-649, 1889)

THE NEED FOR SELF-CRITICAL ANALYSIS

It is dangerous to build confidence in our own righteousness. We should't build faith in ourselves but in God. And that means that a healthy fear of God should lead us to a constant self-criticism and humble examination of our own belief and further progress in the knowledge of the truth about God: "The fear of the LORD is the beginning of wisdom." (Psalm 111:10) If the truth is really important to us, then we will not hesitate to expose it to the criticism of different opinions: "Where there is no guidance the people fall, but in abundance of counselors there is victory." (Proverbs 11:14) Unlike the advocates of the Spiritual formation who make a taboo of each review and declare the words of criticism as hate speech, the spirit of original Protestantism is not afraid of critical examination, but it is precisely based on it. One of the greatest protestant theologies Paul Johannes Tillich (1886 - 1965) claims:

> "The prophetic spirit begins not with the criticism of society but with self-criticism. To be a Protestant is to be critically self-critical. ... Protestantism cannot desire a monopoly or totalitarian control. Human nature being what it is, Protestantism requires external criticism for its own health." (John Leith, Pilgrimage of a Presbyterian, p. 328.)

In the nineteenth century Protestant thinkers and clerics have warned that the blessing of democracy will soon be converted into anarchy, and anarchy into totalitarianism, if the light of prophetic self-criticism would be extinguished.

> "While celebrating American democracy and material progress, Dorchester and Strong worried about the implications of these values. They extolled democracy but warned that democracy unchecked by moral restraint would descend into

anarchy. They rejoiced in material progress but cautioned against materialism. Because America was a set of principles to be realized more than a finished product, loyal Americans could never rest content. In the spirit of the Puritan jeremiad, they needed to engage in ceaseless self-criticism and repentance as a means of corporate rededication to America's destiny." (Jonathan D. Sarna, Minority Faiths and the American Protestant Mainstream)

"The Reformation has favoured the progress of the nations which have adopted it, by permitting them to found free institutions, while Catholicism leads to despotism or anarchy, and often alternately to both. Representative government is the natural government of Protestant populations. Despotic government is the congenial government of Catholic populations. ... Catholics, unable either to found liberty, or to do without it, make despotism necessary, and yet will not submit to it. ... Regulated liberty is not possible without good morals." (Emile De Laveleye, Protestantism and Catholicism in their bearing upon the Liberty and Prosperity of Nations, pp. 30-31, 52, 1876)

"Only a virtuous people are capable of freedom. As nations become corrupt and vicious, they have more need of masters." (Benjamin Franklin)

Ellen G. White (1827 - 1915) has the same spirit of understanding of truth:

"The fact that there is no controversy or agitation among God's people should not be regarded as conclusive evidence that they are holding fast to sound doctrine. There is reason to fear that they may not be clearly discriminating between truth and error. When no new questions are started by investigation of the Scriptures, when no difference of opinion arises which will set men to searching the Bible for themselves to make sure that they have the truth, there will be many now, as in ancient times, who will hold to tradition and worship they know not what. ... I have been shown that many who profess to have a knowledge of present truth know not what they believe. They do not understand the evidences of their faith. ... When separated from those of like faith and compelled to stand singly and alone to explain their belief, they will be surprised to see how confused are their ideas of what they had accepted as truth. ... Agitate, agitate, agitate!" (GW 298-299)

"Satan is fruitful in bringing up devices to evade the truth. But I call upon you to believe the words I speak today. Truth of heavenly origin is confronting Satan's falsehoods, and this truth will prevail....

Opposition and resistance only serve to bring out truth in new, distinct lines. The more truth is spoken against, the brighter it will shine. Thus the precious ore is polished. Every word of slander spoken against it, every misrepresentation of its value, awakens attention, and is the means of leading to closer investigation as to what is saving truth. The truth becomes more highly estimated. New beauty and greater value are revealed from every point of view." (Manuscript 8a, 1888.)

HYPOCRITICAL SELF-CRITICISM WITHOUT ANALYSIS

Often the fruits of wrong belief are so drastic, that its agents are being forced to condemn them. But, since they retain the source of evil in their wrong belief, this self-criticism is hypocritical.

For example, a Catholic priest will, with the story about hell, burden with guilt his believers as a motive of religious zeal, and then, the same believers, he will reprimand for a whole set of weaknesses that are the natural result of burdening with guilt. These are the weaknesses of suspicion (fear of conspiracy), hypocrisy, projection, tendency towards false moral condemnation, gossiping and evil-speaking.

The Orthodox priest will also show the tendency to talk about religious and national values and thus awake religious and national pride in his believers, and then he will hypocritically quote the words of Jesus ***"Love your enemies."***

Why is it hypocritical?

Because a person who is poisoned by pride, because of the pride itself, becomes too sensitive, easily insulted and aggressive. He naturally generates conflicts with his closest friends, so it is illusory to expect that he can love his enemies.

A contemporary Protestant or charismatic preacher will be faced with the expressed emotional lability of his believers, and therefore he will be inclined to preach sermons in which he will emphasize that believers need to put reason above their emotions, and should't let their feelings govern their reason and behavior. But such self-criticism of the lability of believers is hypocritical and completely fruitless, if we bear in mind that the demands of God's law are neglected. Namely, if the selfishness of the human heart is not rebuked by the law, a man will naturally be the slave of his feelings. As long as he is ruled by unreproved selfishness, no matter how much he tries to maintain his feelings under his reason and his will, this selfishness will keep him a slave of emotions.

In the charismatic communities, a preacher can be heard vehemently preaching from the pulpit: "If people come here just because of miracles, they better not come!" Such self-criticism is also hypocritical, because the need for miracles as proof of the reconciliation of believers with God is the natural need of many believers who are not in peace with God because of their non-repentance for their sins. Since they can not be satisfied with the simple faith in God who accepts them, they lower their look of faith from Christ to themselves, and in miracles, feelings, false spiritual gifts and other signs seek proof that they are supposedly with God.

In Protestant communities in which believers seek salvation in each other, in the feeling of mutual closeness and familiarity, the preachers will often sermonize against adultery, not realizing that mass adulteries among believers are a natural fruit of an exaggerated mutual closeness of the believers and their orientation towards each other, instead to God.

Advocates of the Spiritual formation will criticize the various fruits of their unconquered great Ego and all the fruits of seeking salvation in techniques, but such criticism is hypocritical, bearing in mind that they make taboo of each examination and exposition of their beliefs to criticism, fearing that their delusions might be unmasked, and thus they might lose their false peace.

Instead of seeing the cause of their failure in the struggle against temptation in their wrong belief, they try to accuse the unpleasant circumstances for their failure.

ACCUSING THE CIRCUMSTANCES FOR OUR OWN SINFULNESS

Speaking of the representatives of false doctrine - false prophets, Jesus explained that wrong belief brings bad fruit of life:

> "By their fruit you will recognize them. Do people pick grapes from thornbushes, or figs from thistles? Likewise, every good tree bears good fruit, but a bad tree bears bad fruit. A good tree cannot bear bad fruit, and a bad tree cannot bear good fruit. ... Thus, by their fruit you will recognize them." (Matthew 7:16-20)

Therefore, the solution to the problem of every vice and sin is to make people meet God in the right light. Believers whose faith does not bring forth a good fruit should rethink their beliefs and reject the delusions that impede them in the triumph over life's temptations.

But instead of re-examining their belief in the light of God's Word and rejecting their misconceptions, the Spiritual formation leads them to accuse other people and the unpleasant living conditions for their failure in their struggle against vice.

In the "Spiritual Exercises" of Ignatius Loyola, we find the direction of a man to dwell upon the events of his entire life, as well as upon the Original sin (the sin of Adam and Eve):

> *Let the first point be, a certain inquest by which the sins of one's whole life are recalled into the memory, the person going through, step by step, and examining the several years and*

spaces of time. In which thing we are assisted by a threefold summing up, by considering, that is to say, the places where we have lived, the various modes of intercourse we have had with others, and the different kinds of offices or occupations in which we have been engaged. ... The second point is, to exercise the same three powers concerning the sin of our first Parents, which we shall call the second, going over by the memory, how long a penance they underwent on account of it; how great a corruption has invaded the human race; how many thou sands of human beings have been thrust down to hell." (The Spiritual Exercises of St. Ignatius of Loyola, 33, 29-30)

The 12-step program in the first step requires from trainee to explore problems at work or in relationship with other people as the causes of his own vice (Journey to Wholeness, Step 1, page 14). According to this program, the root of man's sinfulness (vice and addiction) is not seen in the separation of man from God, but in his traumas from childhood:

"A second component in our inventory is discovering the roots of our addictions and codependencies. In most cases, this means we have to examine our childhoods. What needs were not met during these years? What negative experiences or messages about ourselves did we absorb in the dysfunction of our families? ... Which of our addictions or controlling behaviors seem to go along with these gaps in our past?" (Journey to Wholeness - Twelve Step Recovery, step 4, page 14)

In the book "Toxic Faith," its author, Jack Felton, lists the entire set of bad fruits of the Spiritual formation, which he criticizes and gives them the term - toxicity. His criticism is hypocritical, because he does not associate the cause with consequence.

He does not reprimand the misconceptions of the Spiritual formation that are the source of such fruits, but as the cause of bad fruits of faith, in addition to the childhood traumas, he also lists strict parents, disappointment and man's low conception of his own value and greatness.

ARE STRICT PARENTS GUILTY?

It is true that strict parents can, by their wrong example, give to the child the wrong conception of God as a tyrant who hates sinners. But it is also true that the liberal upbringing of children results in deviant conscience in those children, which leads them to regard every reasonable criticism of their caprices as a manifestation of tyranny and hatred by the authorities. In the case of spoiled children, statistics could clearly show that those children who are criticized by parents for stealing money, are more prone to depression than those children who do not receive such verbal "torture".

However, regardless of what kind of bad influence it is, in the phase of adolescent independence from parents, a person forms independent thinking and decision-making, imbued by desire to reexamine everything learned. Also, the Holy Spirit through the Bible and through the righteous examples of other people, as well as through personal experience, reveals to a man the proper understanding of God's character. Therefore, man has the freedom to choose, between good and bad influence, a good influence, and to establish personal union with God. Nobody has the excuse to continue to represent the conception of God as a tyrant when the Holy Spirit during his whole life reveals the opposite idea of God, as a God who loves the sinner, but does not love sin.

But people who are not truly reconciled with God because they do not want to reject their sins, have a real concept about the "sword of judgment that hovers above their head".

They consciously or subconsciously know that due to their unrepentance, the eternal death awaits them. They are disturbed because their conscience is really upset, and instead of repenting for their sins, they try to distort the conception of God by throwing out from this conception every element of His righteousness and reproof of the God's Law for their own sins.

They want to convince themselves that they are not under God's condemnation because of their unrepentance and to blame for their real fear of eternal death not themselves, but rather their parents and their former, perhaps, really rude attitude towards them. Under the wrong conception of God, which is a consequence of the parents' strictness, they think of the conception of God through His law. Because they are in a state of unrepentance, their hearts are not pleased with the requirements of God's law as the revelation of God's character, but in the requirements of the law they see the shadow of God's judgment.

"Sounds of terror are in his ears; While at peace the destroyer comes upon him. He does not believe that he will return from darkness, And he is destined for the sword. ... He knows that a day of darkness is at hand. Distress and anguish terrify him, They overpower him like a king ready for the attack..." (Job 15:21-25)

"But there the LORD will give you a trembling heart, failing of eyes, and despair of soul. So your life shall hang in doubt before you; and you will be in dread night and day, and shall have no assurance of your life. In the morning you shall say, 'Would that it were evening!' And at evening you shall say, 'Would that it were morning!' because of the dread of your heart which you dread, and for the sight of your eyes which you will see." (Deuteronomy 28:65-67)

Since they are reprimanded by the law for sins that do not want to leave, the law does not approach them to God, but leads them to hell. That is why they see the solution for their upset conscience in the correction of the conception of God, depriving it from the requirements of the law of God, and not in their repentance.

If such persons, however, in the light of God's law, acknowledge their guilt and die to self, Jesus' sacrifice for their sins does not have to be in vain. If they elevate their look of faith through the Holy Scriptures to the Lord, and sincerely repent of their sins, they will no longer be under the condemnation of the law, and will have no inclination to perceive God as some kind of tyrant because they will no longer be in conflict with Him.

IS A DISAPPOINTMENT GUILTY?

Disappointment is a consequence of thwarted expectations from other people. When our soul's thirst is not satisfied in relationship with God, we come to temptation of trying to satisfy it in relation to other people and in what we normally do (job, leisure). Even the most normal relationships and activities, due to the wrong function which we attach to them, naturally lead us to disappointment in ourselves and others. If we do not have such expectations, we could never be disappointed either by ourselves or others, because we would not expect from ourselves and others what is impossible - to satisfy us. Precisely because troubles can help us to become aware of the wrong function of our relationship with other people, God allows them.

The Bible speaks of troubles as the tool by which God works with sinners:

> "For the Lord disciplines the one he loves, and chastises every son whom he receives. It is for discipline that you have to endure. God is treating you as sons. For what son is there whom his father does not discipline? If you are left without discipline, in which all have participated, then you are illegitimate children and not sons." (Hebrews 12:6-8)

Spiritual writer Ellen G. White explains the meaning of troubles:

> "None who receive God's word are exempt from difficulty and trial; but when affliction comes, the true Christian does not become restless, distrustful, or despondent. ... Through conflict the spiritual life is strengthened. Trials well borne will develop steadfastness of character and precious spiritual graces. The perfect fruit of faith, meekness, and love often matures best amid storm clouds and darkness." (EGW, Christ's Object Lessons, 60) "God permits us to experience the ills of poverty, and places us in difficult positions, that the defects in our characters may be revealed and their asperities be smoothed away." (EGW, 4T, 496)

"Through affliction God reveals to us the plague spots in our characters, that by His grace we may overcome our faults. Unknown chapters in regard to ourselves are opened to us, and the test comes, whether we will accept the reproof and the counsel of God. When brought into trial, we are not to fret and complain. We should not rebel, or worry ourselves out of the hand of Christ. We are to humble the soul before God. The ways of the Lord are obscure to him who desires to see things in a light pleasing to himself. They appear dark and joyless to our human nature. But God's ways are ways of mercy and the end is salvation." (EGW, DA, 301)

God leads us through distresses, which we can maturely endure only if we die to self and our weaknesses. If we cultivate arrogance in our hearts, we are not in a position to peacefully endure humiliation by injustice. If we do not repent of the arrogance, which makes us easily offended, we will have the temptation while enduring injustice to fall into an extra sin - in sin of hatred. If we are selfish or carnal, then any distress that thwarts us in emotional or physical pleasure, provokes in us - the spirit of depression. The selfish need for a feeling of being loved makes us naturally vulnerable and depressive. Unconquered arrogance will naturally make us overly insulting and therefore irritable and frustrating. Our hypocritical tendency to bind our sins in their manifestation can result in fretfulness and the need to project them to other people and then to condemn them. In this way, on the basis of the symptoms of our injured Ego and unclean conscience, we can become aware of the need for our internal reform.

Perhaps we are leading our spiritual struggle on the wrong place, so hard distresses can help us in that case. In the moments of the trial, we will discover whether we truly rely on God or on ourselves. Let us note the words of Jesus about the troubles that will destroy our spiritual building if we build it on the sand, instead of on the Rock, which represents a reliance on ourselves instead of Christ:

"Therefore everyone who hears these words of Mine and acts on them, may be compared to a wise man who built his house on the rock. And the rain fell, and the floods came, and the winds blew and slammed against that house; and yet it did not fall, for it had been founded on the rock. Everyone who hears these words of Mine and does not act on them, will be like a foolish man who built his house on the sand. The rain fell, and the floods came, and the winds blew and slammed against that house; and it fell -- and great was its fall." (Matthew 7:24-27)

According to Jesus' words, trouble is the test of whether we are with God, and according to the representatives of the Spiritual formation, trouble is to blame for our spiritual failures. Instead of blaming the storms of life because they have uncovered that we built our spiritual house on the sand instead of the Rock of Life, we should blame ourselves and our wrong foundations of faith.

How do troubles help us to become aware that we are leading our spiritual battle on the wrong place?

If we only hypocritically bind our sins in manifestation, instead of truly repenting for them, we will be tempted to psychically "break" under the burden of temptation. In this way, the troubles protect us from hypocritical self-control as the wrong solution.

Some persons found their reform of the spirit on the reform of the feelings instead of on the reform of the driving motives of the heart. Such persons will lose their goodness as soon as the stress of life spoils their feelings. Thus they will become aware that they build their spiritual building on the sand, instead of on the Rock, to which the storm of temptation can do nothing.

Hence, troubles guard us from fatal deceiving by provoking us to express our real state of the spirit. Troubles put before us a challenge to conquer ourselves and to grow into mature human personalities or to fall into worse state than before temptation. If we are not conquering the temptations, they will conquer us. By the immature reaction of our will to temptation, we weaken the power of our own will. By yielding to temptation, we harden our heart and deprive it of love. Also, we strengthen the servile powers of the great Ego over our own personality. We benumb the voice of conscience, and we certainly lose a common sense if we excuse our fall with various excuses.

If, however, our look of trust we elevate from ourselves to the Lord, we will, by dwelling upon God, allow Him to deal with us and lead us to repentance and victory over ourselves. If we conquer our temptations trusting in God, this victory will produce a positive reform of our character, and we will then, with clean conscience, rely on God that He will change the course of events in our lives with His divine intervention.

When we overcome the temptation, Satan will no longer be able to claim us as his prey, and God himself can deliver us out of trouble, because trouble has accomplished its purpose.

If we were in conflict with people who did injustice to us, God can invite them to repent or deliver us from their harmful influence. Trust in God and renunciation of ourselves lead us to the position of a special God's blessing.

IS A LOW CONCEPTION OF ONE'S OWN VALUE GUILTY?

Allegedly, people can not understand that God loves them if they have a low awareness of their own value and greatness, and if they can not find the reason for their own love and for God's love for themselves.

However, God loves us with an unselfish love that does not seek the reason and interest for love in the values of the one he loves. The reason why God Himself loves us is not within us, in some of our alleged values, but in Him, in the very nature of the unselfish love by which He loves us, and with whom He calls us to love ourselves and others.

God makes us worthy by the fact that he loves us, but He doesn't have a need, as a carnal heart, to seek the reasons for love in our values so that He can love us. As such, love humiliates human pride, people want to present that God loves them because they are somebody and something worthwhile in His eyes, and that by their values themselves they deserve to be loved, and that God is therefore obligated to love them.

Our natural love is selfish, directed towards values which we see in ourselves and others, or towards feelings that other people provoke in us, and not towards our own and other people's personality.

Hence, when one's own values are violated, a person initiated by selfish love begins to hate himself because he does not have the value in himself so that he can love himself. Then, he could start identifying with the values of the community or with the values of his idol, in order to feel valuable himself.

Only true selfless love, which we find in God, enables us to love both ourselves and others as we really are, sinful and weak. Then we do not love the weaknesses we see in ourselves and others, but we love personalities, our own and others.

According to the principles of the book "Toxic Faith," apostle Paul would have strong reasons for toxic faith, because he considered himself to be the worst of all sinners (1 Timothy 1:15) and the smallest of all saints (Ephesians 3: 8). The same could be said for the entire series of Biblical heroes of faith who, in encounter with God, became aware of the very unpleasant perceptions of themselves:

Prophet Isaiah: "Then said I, Woe is me! for I am undone; because I am a man of unclean lips, ... for mine eyes have seen the King, the Lord of hosts." (Isaiah 6:5)

Prophet Daniel: "And I Daniel alone saw the vision: for the men that were with me saw not the vision; but a great quaking fell upon them, so that they fled to hide themselves." (Daniel 10:7-8)

Apostle Peter: "When Simon Peter saw it, he fell down at Jesus' knees, saying, Depart from me; for I am a sinful man, O Lord." (Luke 5:8)

Apostle John: "And when I saw him, I fell at his feet as dead. And he laid his right hand upon me, saying unto me, Fear not; I am the first and the last:" (Revelation 1:17)

The message to Laodicea has not for the purpose to make us toxic believers, because it makes us aware of our own worthlessness, but to heal us from our dangerous self-satisfaction with ourselves:

"I know your deeds, that you are neither cold nor hot. I wish you were either one or the other! So, because you are lukewarm, and neither cold nor hot, I will spew you out of my mouth. You say, 'I am rich; I have acquired wealth and do not need a thing.' But you do not realize that you are wretched, pitiful, poor, blind and naked." (Revelat. 3:15-17)

The low awareness of our own value is a natural consequence of the knowledge of the sublime God's character.

"No deep-seated love for Jesus can dwell in the heart that does not realize its own sinfulness. The soul that is transformed by the grace of Christ will admire His divine character; but if we do not see our own moral deformity, it is unmistakable evidence that we have not had a view of the beauty and excellence of Christ. The less we see to esteem in ourselves, the more we shall see to esteem in the infinite purity and loveliness of our Saviour." (EGW, SC 65)

"We are justified by faith. The soul who understands the meaning of these words will never be self-sufficient." (EGW 6BC 1073)

"...Thus it is with the truly righteous man. He is unconscious of his goodness and piety." (EGW, The Sanctified Life, 13)

"The True Witness declares that when you suppose you are really in a good condition of prosperity you are in need of everything." (EGW, 3T 257)

"While you look higher than yourself, you will have a continual sense of the weakness of humanity. The less you cherish self, the more distinct and full will be your comprehension of the excellence of your Saviour." (EGW, The Desire of Ages, 493)

"It is only he who knows himself to be a sinner that Christ can save. ... We must know our real condition, or we shall not feel our need of Christ's help. We must understand our danger, or we shall not flee to the refuge. We must feel the pain of our wounds, or we should not desire healing." (EGW, Christ's Object Lessons, 158)

This consciousness of our own weakness, sinfulness and worthlessness has the purpose for us to give up our confidence in ourselves and to become confident in God and His character by trusting in Him. Although then we maintain the awareness of our own sinfulness, we do not fall into discouragement with ourselves, because we do not expect anything from ourselves. Since we do not believe in ourselves, we already believe in God, and we can not be disappointed with ourselves. And as we do not rely on ourselves, our sinfulness has no power over us.

If you really believe in God, then it doesn't matter anymore what you are by nature, but it is important what God is like in whom you believe. Then we rely no longer on ourselves and our sinful nature, so our nature has no longer power over us:

"But I say, walk by the Spirit, and you will not gratify the desires of the flesh." (Galatians 5:16) "And those who are in the flesh cannot please God. However, you are not in the flesh but in the Spirit, if indeed the Spirit of God dwells in you. But if anyone does not have the Spirit of Christ, he does not belong to Him. Now if Christ is in you, the body is dead because of sin, but the Spirit is life because of righteousness." (Romans 8:4-10) "No one who abides in Him sins; no one who sins has seen Him or knows Him." (1 John 3:6)

Therefore, if a low idea of our own worth leads us to discouragement with ourselves, instead of "clinging" to Jesus, it is a sure indication that we believe in ourselves and not in God, and that our foundations of faith are wrong.

So, we can conclude - if a person is unsuccessful in conquering temptation, it is not a solution to justify his failure by referring to bad external influences or a low idea about his own value and grandeur, but in re-examining, acknowledging and rejecting the mistakes that made him lead the spiritual struggle in a wrong level.

ARE THE UNMET BASIC NEEDS GUILTY?

One of the excuses for failure on the spiritual level, which can also be heard, is referring to the unmet basic needs of life, which allegedly disable a man to successfully fight against his sins and have peace and happiness in God. In Program 12 steps, we read an excuse for postponing the spiritual struggle until these needs are met:

"Waiting to make decisions or to move in any direction until we have met our basic needs is always a good way to avoid further pitfalls and potholes." (Journey to Wholeness - Twelve Step Recovery, step 1, page 25)

Psychologist Julian Melgosa cites Maslow's pyramid of human needs, claiming that the satisfaction of existential and psychological needs is necessary for a man in order to avoid stress. With this understanding, Julian Melgosa leads people to blame, for their immature reaction to stress, not their separation from God, but the unsatisfaction of those needs which are largely the consequence of man's separation from God.

Spiritually unsatisfied person, in his attempt to satisfy himself out of God, naturally abuses his existential needs (for example, the need for food by becoming voracious). Sexual abilities, instead of remaining only abilities for expressing love and also for making offspring, become driving motive when starting to be used for the sake of satisfaction. By putting other people in the place of God, a man also forms psychological needs in relation to other people, which we call selfishness. If a man abuses the image of his own value and greatness, he forms psychological need for the feeling of his own value and greatness which we call vanity. All these distorted needs, that are by-product of the separation of a man from God, the bearers of the Spiritual formation want to present as if they were real human needs.

Psychological needs are the main initiator of pseudo-spiritual experience. But, between the psychological need for satisfaction and the real spiritual need for salvation in God, there are fundamental differences.

One thing is the need of the Pharisee, because of which he goes to the temple and fulfills religious obligations, and the other is the need of a tax collector who begs God for mercy. In Jesus' story of two supplicants in the temple, both supplicants, both the Pharisee and the tax collector, left the temple very satisfied, but while the Pharisee was moved by psychological need, the tax collector was moved by real spiritual need:

"Two men went up to the temple to pray, one a Pharisee and the other a tax collector. The Pharisee, standing by himself, was praying thus:

'God, I thank you that I am not like other people: thieves, rogues, adulterers, or even like this tax collector. I fast twice a week; I give a tenth of all my income.'

But the tax collector, standing far off, would not even look up to heaven, but was beating his breast and saying, 'God, be merciful to me, a sinner!'

I tell you, this man went down to his home justified rather than the other; for all who exalt themselves will be humbled, but all who humble themselves will be exalted." (Luke 18:10-14)

Although the Pharisee and the tax collector expressed their needs to God who had the same name, although they both came out of the temple very pleased, there was, however, a fundamental difference between them. Both of them went away satisfied, but as the Pharisee went away satisfied with himself - with his own character, the tax collector left satisfied with God - with the character of God who forgave his sins. The tax collector did not have a need to be satisfied with himself, nor he could be it, for he was completely satisfied with God, His grace which forgives sins and renews human hearts. And that was enough for him.

Unlike the tax collector, the Pharisee could not be satisfied with God when he was in conflict with Him due to his unrepentance. A Pharisee wrongly interpreted the demands of God's law, as if law only rebukes wrong behavior or bad feelings, and not the bad motives of the heart, so he deceived himself with his formal correctness and his pleasant feelings, while his heart remained unreformed. Because of the superficial moral criteria, he was not aware that his heart was still under the power of sin. But as he had no clear conscience because of it, he could not be satisfied with simple faith in God. That is why he lowered the view of the faith from the God's face to himself, in order to become satisfied with himself. Unclean conscience formed a need for the feeling of his own righteousness. The unsatisfied spiritual need for God formed in him - what psychologists call - a psychological need. By paying attention to his good deeds, he satisfied the psychological need for the feeling of his own righteousness.

Spiritual need is a need for the reform of the heart motives under the influence of the Holy Spirit and for the reconciliation of man with God through the merits of Jesus Christ, while the psychological need is a need not for the reform of the heart motives, but for the reform of the feelings by which a person will suppress the awareness of the need for the reform of the motives of the heart.

Psychological needs find their fulfillment in the realization of certain feelings, in contrast to the spiritual needs which find their fulfillment in the realization of a certain spiritual state (in changing of the essential motives). Because of their essential difference, psychological and spiritual needs are mutually opposed by their goals: the psychological need is intended to inebriate and suppress the man's awareness of his problem, while the spiritual need is an expression of reasonable awareness of the need for change of the man's condition.

Spiritual need is analogous to the need of a sick man for a physician who will heal him at the root, while the psychological need is analogous to the need of a sick man to eliminate the consequences of his illness (feeling of pain, exhaustion, etc.). As the pain pill does not remove the cause of the disease, so the response to a psychological need does not solve the essence of the human spiritual problem. It is necessary to go to the doctor and solve the problem at the root.

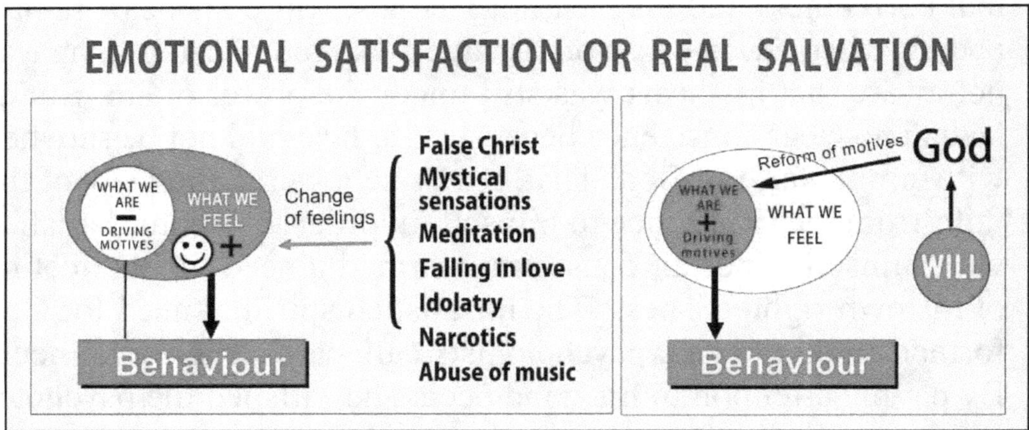

Will we believe in the man's claim that he is healthy, if he says, "I'm healthy, but I still have to take painkillers!" The need for a pill reveals that the problem is not resolved. Psychological needs reveal an unresolved problem at the spiritual level. Although many people work for years to "solve" their spiritual problem, they actually aim to achieve a certain feeling, and not a specific spiritual condition (correct character and peace with God).

Unlike the Holy Ghost who makes us conscious of our spiritual poverty (Matthew 5:3) and of dependence upon God, the poisonous wine of Babylon is the system of the wrong religion that suffocates this awareness of the need for God. As the Pharisees interpreted the Holy Scriptures in a way that is pleasing to the human nature, so do many Christians today.

"But the Bible is interpreted in a manner that is pleasing to the unrenewed heart, while its solemn and vital truths are made of no effect. Love is dwelt upon as the chief attribute of God, but it is degraded to a weak sentimentalism, making little distinction between good and evil." (EGW DD 22.2)

Pleasant feelings and experiences are proclaimed by many as the criterion of the true spiritual path and the indicator of the successful realization of the meaning of one's own life. In order to gain the approval of the majority, the representatives of the Spiritual formation, mainly Christian psychologists, with their advices flatter the vain need of a man to feel special and very valuable, as they also indulge the selfish need of a man for inebriating with feelings. They want to show that there is nothing wrong with satisfying "natural" human needs, as they call satisfaction of unrenewed motives of a fallen human nature.

In order to calm their conscience, they often quote Maslow's pyramid of needs, which lists sinful and self-righteous human needs into the man's existential and psychological needs. According to the Maslow's pyramid of needs, primary human needs include the need for existence and security. The primary needs are followed by the needs for belonging (for feeling of being loved) and esteem, and at the very top of the pyramid there is a need for self-actualization, which also includes the sphere of human spirituality.

The first problem of such a division is the fact that Maslow, in the natural needs, places not only a man's real needs, but also those irrational needs which, speaking in the language of psychology, are the result of fixations due to the immaturity of personality, or which, speaking in terms of spirituality, are sinful and self-righteous human needs - the fruit of the separation of man from God.

Every kind of voraciousness and greed, as well as obsession with sex, can have a cover for their existence in the primary needs of Maslow's pyramid, while emotional and social immaturity, the abuse of other people for psychological and emotional satisfaction, as well as personal arrogance and pride, have an excuse in the higher spheres of Maslow's pyramid of human needs. It is incomprehensible that Christian psychologists, quoting the Maslow's pyramid of human needs, provide themselves and others with an excuse for those human needs that are the fruit of separation of man from God and substitute God with false gods.

The second problem is the assertion that a person is not able to meet his higher needs if his lower needs are not met. According to the Maslow's pyramid, a man's need for God is in the last place, and appears allegedly only when his other needs are met. The misconception is worse when it comes to remembering that those remaining needs, which precede the need for God, can always remain unmet precisely because they contain in themselves the sinful needs that are insatiable. All these needs of the Maslow's pyramid present a temptation for man to seek in them the satisfaction of his soul instead of in God:

> "For all that is in the world, the lust of the flesh and the lust of the eyes and the boastful pride of life, is not from the Father, but is from the world." (1 John 2:16)

> "And make no provision for the flesh in regard to its lusts." (Romans 13:14)

If a man needs to wait to satisfy his need for pleasure, for approval of the surroundings, and for his own value and greatness so that he could, only after that, become ready to seek for God and choose Him, then he is waiting for impossible. These needs are insatiable, so therefore the Bible for the sources of happiness of this world says that they can not hold the water and can not satiate:

> "Be appalled, O heavens, at this, And shudder, be very desolate," declares the LORD. For My people have committed two evils: They have forsaken Me, The fountain of living waters, To hew for themselves cisterns, Broken cisterns That can hold no water." (Jeremiah 2:12-13)

> "Why do you spend money for what is not bread, And your wages for what does not satisfy?" (Isaiah 55:2)

It is precisely when he managed to satisfy his sinful and self-righteous needs, a man would realize that he needs no longer the biblical God, because he would find a substitute for Him in meeting all other needs of the Maslow's pyramid of needs.

Instead of Maslow's pyramid of needs which excuses the sinful needs of human nature, it would be more correct to understand the real pyramid of human needs that divides human needs into three spheres: the sphere of existence, the sphere of need for the fulfillment of the meaning and the sphere of relationship of our personality with God. Existential needs are very little demanding and by their fulfillment they allow a man to fulfill higher needs, and those are the needs of the meaning of one's own life.

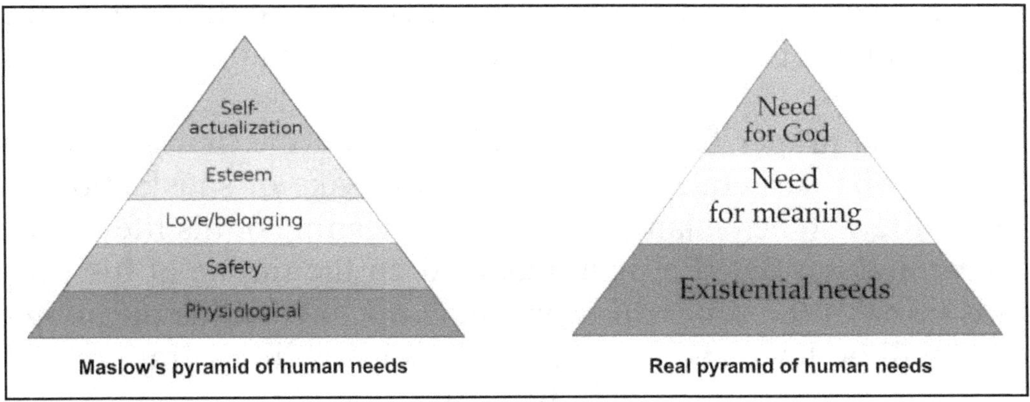

We can notice that in real life, in contrast to the Maslow's pyramid, the meaning of life is more important to a man than his existence, so he will show readiness to endanger existence and even sacrifice his own life, in order to fulfill the meaning of his life, no matter if that meaning is good or bad.

A man will show willingness to sacrifice his own life for the life of another man or to endanger his own health and life to enjoy the hedonism, or to die in the battle out of hatred due to his insulted proud Ego.

Contrary to the classical view that the only purpose of the organism's ability is - its existence, we see that organisms live not only to survive, but also to fulfill the meaning of their existence. Man is not only created to survive, but to serve others. His ability to create, sing, play on a violin, celebrate God and serve other living beings far exceed his ability to survive. That is why we distinguish the existential abilities of the first sphere that serve only for survival, from the ability of the middle spheres which serve to fulfill the meaning of life.

Man has the freedom to choose the meaning of his existence, whether to use his abilities to serve others or to misuse those abilities for the sake of satisfaction. Which purpose will have his needs from the middle sphere depends on the fulfillment of the needs of the highest sphere, upon the person's relationship with God. If a man is independent from the true God, he will have to put false gods on the throne of his heart. His spiritual need will not be met, and he will abuse the existential abilities as well as the abilities of the sphere of meaning to seek in them a substitute for God.

As the proper function of abilities from the first and second spheres be desecrated by abuse for the sake of satisfaction, his very life will be endangered, and the meaning of his life become meaningless. But if a man puts God on the throne of his heart, his thirst of the soul will be satisfied in God and his meaning of life will be love, and it means that all his abilities from the first and the second spheres will be in function of the response to the real needs of life (his own needs, the needs of other people and humanity).

TWO BASIC DECEPTIONS AS A CAUSE OF WEAKNESS TO OVERCOME TEMPTATION - WRONG UNDERSTANDING OF THE CONCEPT OF LOVE AND THE SPIRIT OF THE GOD'S LAW

There are two basic misconceptions that are the source of the failure of people who intend to conquer their vice.

The first misconception is the ignorance of God and the character of His love, due to the natural orientation towards oneself, instead towards God. The result of this misconception is that people, instead of God, seek for the victory over the vice in themselves - in the motives of their own sinful nature and unclean conscience.

Instead of being moved to repentance by the revelation of God's love which leads to repentance, they repent for their vice driven by the *fear* of unclean conscience, the *shame* of insulted pride and the sadness of the *selfish sentiment*.

Such people sincerely believe that on repentance they are moved by real love, and actually they are driven by motives of their own sinful nature and their own unclean conscience.

Their conception of God, which is not the fruit of God's revelation through the Bible, but is the fruit of projection of one's own sinful motives to God, prompts those motives of their nature instead of reprimanding them.

They do not distinguish the righteousness of divine origin from their own human righteousness, just as those of which the apostle Paul writes:

"For I bear them record that they have a zeal of God, but not according to knowledge. For they being ignorant of God's righteousness, and going about to establish their own righteousness, have not submitted themselves unto the righteousness of God." (Romans 10:2-3)

As such people repent out of bad motives, their repentance remains without God's response.

Another misconception is the ignorance of the meaning and spirit of God's law, which results in the unconsciousness of one's own sins and the deceit of conscience by formal correction of behavior or the reform of one's own feelings.

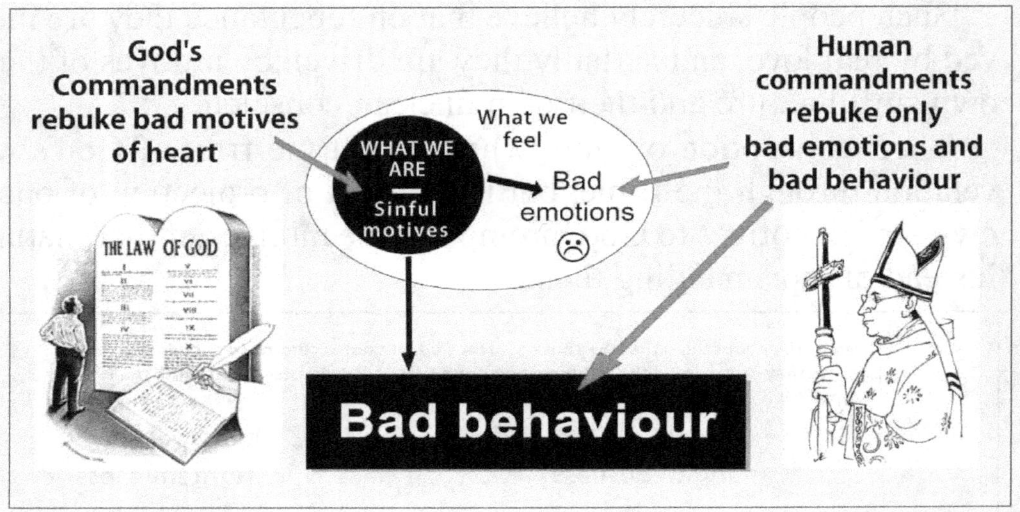

Jesus explains that a vain is religion which is the result of human criteria of good and evil:

"They worship Me in vain, teaching as doctrines the commands of men. Disregarding the command of God, you keep the tradition of men. He also said to them, You completely invalidate God's command in order to maintain your tradition!" (Mark 7:7-9)

Apostle Paul reveals that without law he is not conscious of sin:

"I would not have known what is to covet if the law had not said You shall not covet." (Romans 7:7)

The purpose of the law is "that sin by the commandment might become exceeding sinful." (Romans 7:13) "Since through the law comes knowledge of sin." (Romans 3:20) Without knowing the requirements of the law, people are naturally unaware of their sin. They do not repent of sinful desires at the level of the motives of their own heart, but only for the unpleasant symptoms of sinful desires in their thoughts, feelings and actions. A man will sincerely repent because he said a bad word to his friend, but not for he is such in his heart (because he is not aware of his sinfulness). He most often repents only because he has allowed his sin to manifest, but not for the sinful motive of the heart itself.

Psychiatrist Torben Bergland, in his sermon advocates that a person can only repent for his own bad actions, but not for what he himself is (state of mind, bad motives of the heart):

"You can repent of doing something wrong, but you can not repent because you have defects, because you are what you are." (Torben Bergland, Prophecy, Nis, September 16, 2017) This understanding we also find in the 12-step program:

"We are not our problems. We are created with hope and promise, and are not limited to the detours and obstacles we encounter. Realizing this will help us hold our problems at arm's length, to separate our identity from our behavior. Our problem is not who we are, but what methods we have used to cope with life's stresses, or to protect us from physical and emotional pain. ... What thought patterns or behaviors might I label as a problem in my life? How long would I guess I have struggled with this problem?" (Journey to Wholeness - Twelve Step Recovery, step 3, page 22)

Instead of dying to oneself and reforming the essential heart motives, the "solution" of the problem of sinful desires can be seen in their redirecting to a "healthy" way of manifestation. Therefore, besides the notion of *"healthy lust"*, we have concepts such as *"healthy arrogance", "healthy selfishness", "healthy sloth", "healthy self-pity", "healthy greed", "healthy impatience," etc.* (Journey to Wholeness - Twelve Step Recovery, step 4, page 28).

Of course, in such a concept of salvation, there is no real need of man for God, who transforms the human heart, but only a need for support in his own self-control. Often people are struggling against bad thoughts, however, the problem remains because the source of sinful thoughts is in unreformed human heart:

"And He was saying, That which proceeds out of the man, that is what defiles the man. For from within, out of the heart of men, proceed the evil thoughts, fornications, thefts, murders, adulteries, deeds of coveting and wickedness, as well as deceit, sensuality, envy, slander, pride and foolishness. All these evil things proceed from within and defile the man." (Mark 7:20-23)

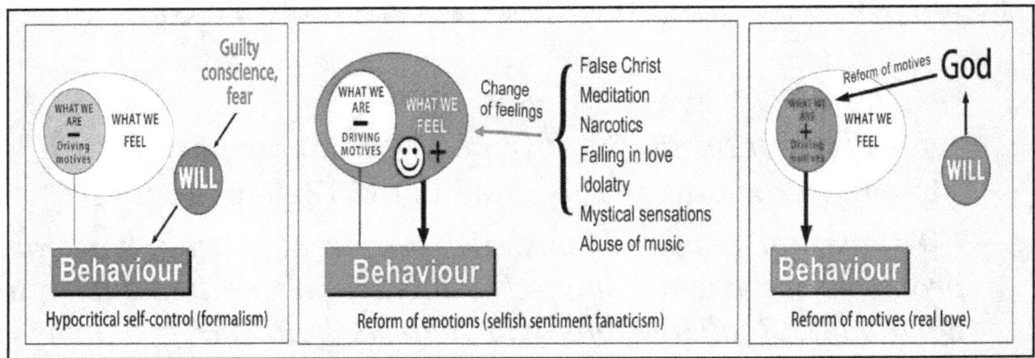

As they do not repent for the sinful desire itself, but only for its destructive way of manifestation and satisfaction, their prayers remain without God's response. They are only disturbed with the consequences of sin, and not the sin itself. To such a cry of their soul Satan has the right to obsess them and to cause them supernatural sensations that suffocate awareness of their real problem.

As their conscience is not pure, they become burdened with proof that they are with God, a proof which they seek in their feelings, miracles, false spiritual gifts and various other signs. They can not be pleased with the simple faith in God that He accepts them, when they are in conflict with God by their own unrepentance for the iniquity of their hearts.

"There are many whose religion consists in theory. To them a happy emotion is godliness. They say, "Come to Jesus, and believe in him. It makes no difference what you believe so long as you are honest in your belief." They do not seek to make the sinner understand the true character of sin. ...There are many professedly sanctified ones who are aiding Satan in his work. They talk much of feeling; they speak of their love for

God. But God does not recognize their love; for it is a delusion of the enemy. God has given these persons light, but they have refused to accept it. With the father of lies, they will receive the reward of disobedience. It had been better for them not to have known the way of righteousness than after they had known it to turn from the holy commandment delivered unto them." (EGW, Review and herald June 26, 1900)

To make people aware of true character of their sins, God sends specific messages to mankind. He intends to make them aware of the need to rely on God instead of themselves, and to repent for the sins of the heart and not just for the symptoms of sin in thoughts, feelings and acts.

Four temptations of modern (fallen) Protestantism and Charismatic movement

The bad motives of religious zeal:
Selfish sentiment instead of love

Spiritual struggle in the wrong plan:
Criterion of love is not God's law, but feelings

System of deluding of an unclear conscience:
Unclean conscience is calmed by feelings, miracles and signs

Renunciation of reasonable questioning through:
The feelings of one's own heart are authority

Without specific messages, people would not become conscious of the need for salvation in Christ. Let us remember the example of the message by which John the Baptist was preparing the Jewish people to recognize in Jesus Jesus the Savior of sin:

"Before the seed of the gospel could find lodgment, the soil of the heart must be broken up. Before they would seek healing from Jesus, they must be awakened to their danger from the wounds of sin. God does not send messengers to flatter the sinner. He delivers no message of peace to lull the unsanctified into fatal security. He lays heavy burdens upon the conscience of the wrongdoer, and pierces the soul with arrows of conviction. The ministering angels present to him the fearful judgments of God to deepen the sense of need, and prompt the cry, "What must I do to be saved?" Then the hand that has humbled in the dust, lifts up the penitent. The voice that has rebuked sin, and put to shame pride and ambition, inquires with tenderest sympathy, "What wilt thou that I shall do unto thee?" (E.G.White, DA 104)

Every message from God is an adequate response to the temptation of the one to whom it is addressed. It has the ultimate purpose that, by unmasking their idols and false objects of confidence (techniques and feelings), make them aware that Christ is their only savior. The message to the world is the Three Angels' Messages (leaving Babylon of the false doctrines - Revelation 14:6-12; 18:2-4), while the message for the church is - the message to Laodicea (a rebuke for relying on ourselves - Revelation 3:15-17).

In contrast to the messages of God's prophets which make people aware of sins and a need for God as Savior from sins, the message of false prophets, by their flattering content, suppresses the people's need for God:

"From prophet to priest, everyone deals falsely. They have treated My people's brokenness superficially, claiming, "Peace, peace," when there is no peace." (Jeremiah 6:13-14)

Various psychological techniques provide such peace by which a man only suffocates the awareness of the need for God. Psychology was created at the time of the beginning of the decadence of Western civilization, when people had already had very high standards of peace and maturity, as a result of the period of the Protestant Reformation. Peace and maturity, with which the Protestants reacted to the difficult life temptations such as sudden loss of acquired assets or loneliness, or to the life-threatening moments, evoked admiration among non-Protestant nations.

But from the beginning of the decadence of the Protestant world since the mid-nineteenth century, there was a need of people to achieve such high standards of peace by various psychological techniques that do not require renunciation of sin and reconciliation with God. Such techniques should be the subject of our criticism more than the techniques of achieving peace through Catholic indulgences and confession of sins to the priest at the time of Martin Luther.

Modern techniques of inebriating with popular music, yoga and meditation produce a greater blockade of the frontal lobe of the brain responsible for self-assessment, judgment and control, than all Catholic rituals could achieve together.

The shifting of responsibility from ourselves to another culprit (for example, to the bad influence of parents) for our own sinful reactions, is the favorite way of liberation from responsibility and suppressing the soul's need for the merits of Jesus' blood. If the mediation of saints, icons and sculptures is a sin precisely because they provide a psychological consolation with which a person suffocates the need for God, how the greater sin is to induce people to seek salvation one in another, in the misuse of the feelings of closeness (familiarity), in the abuse of music, or whatever psychological consolation?!

Right consolation can only be the correct knowledge of the character of God who is worthy of trust, while the consolation by evoked feelings only suffocates awareness of the need for the reform of the heart's motives and in this way it suppresses the soul's need for God as the Savior.

Without adequate messages people will not lead their spiritual struggle properly, which will result in failure and disappointment. And such failure and disappointment opens the door for deception with the false spiritual experience that comes from the demons and their wonders at the level of experiences and feelings.

On the basis of the delusion that hinders true repentance, the true victory over the vice is impossible. It will not help if we pour new wine into old wineskins. The spiritual building, built on the sand instead on the rock, in the first following temptation,will collapse again.

CONCLUSION ABOUT IMPORTANCE OF CONCEPTION OF GOD

All of the aforementioned misconceptions of the Spiritual formation are the result of the lifting up of the authority of the one's own Ego and the focusing of man on himself instead of God. But the continuous dwelling upon God is not enough, if the conception of God's character is incorrect. If the conception of God is deprived of the requirements of the law, one can, due to the wrong idea about God, to nourish and elevate the authority of the great Ego, because he will come to God from the sinful motives of his nature and draw from them strength for religious zeal. He will most sincerely pray to God to satisfy his sinful desires, instead of begging for relief from them. **But if the conception of God's law correctly defined God's character, the believer will come to God rebuked for his sinful desires.** He will come to God, not *from* sinful motives, but *with* sinful motives, as a burden that torments him, and will sincerely cry to God for the sake of liberation from them.

For three years and a half of His work on Earth, Jesus Christ preached the spirit of the law. When people realized that God's law rebukes their state of spirit and sinful desires, they became ready to, as poor in spirit, receive promised blessing. The awareness that they deserved a death due to their transgressions, made Christ's redemption their vital necessity. The awareness that they are the rebels against God and under the power of sin, made them aware of the need for the Holy Spirit who can give them peace and the experience of spiritual new birth. Completely satisfied with God and His work of salvation, they became relieved of the need to dwell upon themselves and liberated from psychological techniques to additionally work on their salvation:

"When the earth is lightened with the glory of God, we shall see a work similar to that which was wrought when the disciples, filled with the Holy Spirit, proclaimed the power of a risen Saviour. The light of heaven penetrated the darkened minds of those who had been deceived by the enemies of Christ, and the false representation of Him was rejected; for through the efficiency of the Holy Spirit they now saw Him exalted to be a Prince and Saviour, to give repentance unto Israel, and remission of sins. They saw Him encircled with the glory of heaven, with infinite treasures in His hands to bestow upon those who turn from their rebellion. As the apostles set forth the glory of the Only Begotten of the Father, three thousand souls were pricked to the heart, and they were made to see themselves as they were, sinful and polluted, and Christ as their Saviour and Redeemer. Christ was lifted up, Christ was glorified, through the power of the Holy Spirit resting upon men. By the eye of faith these believers saw Him as the one who had borne humiliation, suffering, and death, that they might not perish, but have everlasting life. As they looked upon His spotless righteousness, they saw their own deformity and pollution, and were filled with godly fear, with love and adoration for Him who gave His life a sacrifice for them. They humbled their souls to the very dust, and repented of their wicked works, and glorified God for His salvation...." (EGW, Review and Herald, 22. i 29. nov. 1892)

CONTENT